A New Way To Change Jobs

The Professional Job Changing System

For professionals seeking $50,000 to $1,000,000+

Robert J. Gerberg

Advanced Career Technologies

World Headquarters
7979 E. Tufts Avenue Parkway, Suite 1400, Denver, CO 80237
www.worldwidecareerpartners.com
Call 1-877-628-4496 or email
publisher@www.worldwidecareerpartners.com

CHANGING
THE WAY YOU
THINK ABOUT
HOW TO FIND
THE RIGHT JOB

The Professional Job Changing System. Copyright © 2009, 2010 by C.A.N. Inc. All rights reserved. Design of major illustrations by William F. Sterling. Overall book design and desktop publishing by Paula J. Berge. No part of this book may be used or reproduced in any manner whatsoever, except in the case of brief quotations in articles and reviews. Second edition publication date January 1, 2010. Library of Congress Control Number: 2009910453. ISBN 978-0-578-03991-6. Published by Advanced Career Technologies, 7979 East Tufts Avenue Parkway, Suite 1400, Denver, CO 80237 • 1-877-628-4496 • Fax 1-877-470-9540 • publisher@www.worldwidecareerpartners.com.

Printed and bound in China.

Welcome to the new world of personal marketing.

This book will lead you to "rethink" what you believe about job hunting. More importantly, if you use it to run your search... and reasonably follow this system, you will give yourself a significant competitive advantage.

You will also be able to search with greater speed and confidence, experience less strain... and develop more activity than conventional job hunting approaches would provide. In short, you'll be able to increase your chances for success. To be successful today, you have to make sure you address the 10 major mistakes that can derail your search and lead to failure. Look the following list over carefully and see if any of these apply to you. Then, as you go through this text, you'll learn how to avoid the common mistakes that set others back.

The 10 major mistakes most job hunters make.

- They rely on old methods and don't follow a plan.
- The don't minimize the impact of their liabilities.
- They never fully market all their transferable skills.
- They don't uncover exciting new industry alternatives.
- They present themselves with average resumes.
- They don't have a personal marketing website.
- Their interviewing and negotiating skills are average.
- They don't know how to find enough suitable openings.
- They don't ever contact their best prospects.
- They never uncover leads to emerging jobs.

This system is customized for clients of our divisions that assist professionals and executives who are making a job change. For those who are not our clients, it shares what we've learned over the last several years of working with tens of thousands of job seekers, acquaints you with the invaluable principles of personal marketing, and gives you a clear path for running a much more effective job campaign.

"The only things you regret are the things you don't do."
                                          —Michael Curtiz

"Normal is not something to aspire to."   *—Jody Foster*

"Everybody lives for something better to come."   *—Anonymous*

50% of all professionals never distribute more than 100 resumes. Why?

We all want to believe we are special and that the job market will recognize that. But, it doesn't work that way. Of those who distribute a relatively small number of resumes, less than 3% find a new job. The few that get new jobs are either fortunate enough to have referrals, are triple A+ candidates, or accept jobs that are just "okay." They "don't do much," because they don't understand the market and how to approach it.

87% of all professionals uncover only 3% of the opportunities that are suitable for them. Why?

They fail to directly contact decision makers at growth firms or other employers who are good prospects for them. They don't seek out leads to emerging jobs. They generally network on a limited basis only, without taking advantage of a personal marketing website. They go to relatively few recruiters. And, they uncover only a small percentage of the published openings that are suitable for them.

Only 1 in 10 job seekers... knows how to sell themselves effectively in interviews. Why?

Too many people take interviewing for granted. They never stop to analyze the process from an employer's viewpoint, and don't realize that other good candidates are under consideration. Nine out of every 10 job seekers need 17 or more telephone or face-to-face interviews to close a single offer. Worse yet, some come away with no offers at all.

Superior job hunting depends 30% on formal credentials... and 70% on marketing effort. Why?

It's well known that people with the best formal credentials don't automatically get the best jobs. That's because you have to get your credentials in front of the people who have the best jobs available, or who can create jobs. When they fail to do this, just like everyone else, many of the most marketable people never realize their true potential. Job hunting is a unique situation where a C+ candidate who markets himself well... can end up better than someone with straight "A"s.

Table of Contents

About the author

Bob Gerberg is among America's foremost authorities on professional job hunting. More than 7 million copies of his publications are in circulation. His ideas have been instrumental in helping millions of people who have looked for new positions. Over 25 years he has authored dozens of books.

These have included *The Professional Job Hunter's Guide, An Easier Way to Change Jobs, Sixty Great Letters Which Won New Jobs, $100,000 and Above—The New Realities of Executive Job Hunting, 15 New Rules for Job Hunting Success* and many others.

He has also published *The Career Advancement Series...* a package of 28 booklets and programs consisting of sixteen audios. These include *TAPIT, The Personal Marketing Program, The Executive Job Changing System* and others. Hundreds of thousands of these have been used in outplacement programs by institutions ranging from the U.S. Marine Corps, the CIA, major universities and numerous Fortune 1000 corporations.

Initially with GE before becoming a U.S. Air Force officer, Bob was briefly with Honeywell before starting his career with major food companies, including positions as VP of Marketing Services and Assistant to the Chairman of a Fortune 500 firm. Active in the career field for over two decades, he licensed a system for executive job searches to career firms worldwide... from 1987 to 1997.

With the emergence of the Internet, he was the architect of a new approach to finding positions... a system now used by all divisions of the firm's parent company. Through JMAC (Job Market Access Center), the firm focuses on pioneering technology breakthroughs that make job hunting easier. Other divisions include an e'cruiting division, a global resume writing service and firms specializing in management of job campaigns and senior executive outplacement.

These divisions are contacted by more than 1,200,000 professionals each year. More than 15,000 people are also engaged in private discussions each month. These first-hand experiences are the basis for the many statistics cited in this text. Mr. Gerberg has a B.A. from Colgate University, a year of studies in the United States Air Force, an M.B.A. from the University of Pittsburgh and advanced studies at MIT, sponsored by PepsiCo.

Let's start by recognizing why things have changed.

Since most of us rarely look for a job, we never really develop any expertise at marketing ourselves. In fact, *how to find the right new job* is something that we assume we all know how to do.

Traditional job hunting is no longer effective. Why? Too many people still look for new jobs the same way they did in the 80s and 90s. They start by preparing a single historical resume that says, *"here lies John Doe, he went to these schools, he had these jobs and these achievements."* Then they just start answering ads, networking some friends, contacting a few recruiters and posting their resumes on the Internet. It's hard to believe, but that's all that tens of millions of people still do. Today, much more is needed.

> *"If you do what you've always done, you'll get what you've always gotten."—Anonymous*

What happened to make job hunting so complicated? In 2009, with close to historic unemployment, concern about finding new jobs was discussed in virtually every major newspaper and business magazine. Statistics indicate that beyond those unemployed, another 50% are not considered unemployed... because they had given up or taken part time jobs.

Besides the economy, here's what made things so competitive. The growth of the Internet alone has changed forever the magnitude of resumes in circulation. Combined with the ability to use PCs, faxes and emails, people now distribute many millions of resumes—*each week*. That's a relatively new phenomenon.

Why are there so many people always in the market? Today, employers routinely go through staff reductions. This has led to declining employee loyalty. The concept of long-term employment has largely disappeared from the American landscape.

Now, people change jobs on an average of once every four years. Another factor is that people are living and working considerably longer... either full time or part time. Competition has been boosted enormously by the emergence of thousands of job boards. Many people now leave their resumes posted online—even after they accept new positions.

So, in today's job market, we have both active and passive job seekers whose resumes are available to employers. One major job board now claims that 80 million resumes are in their database—which they market to employers as a recruiting tool.

The bottom line is that we now have a level of competition that is little understood, which was unimaginable just a decade ago. At least ***30 million resumes are circulating at any moment. The jobs available are sizeable, but only a fraction of that number.*** To succeed in a job search today, you must first have an understanding of today's new job market and how it works. Then, you will need to get connected to the openings, leads and contacts you require, and get your credentials read by employers who are high probability prospects for you.

Marketing yourself is actually quite simple, but you must get your credentials into play on a fairly large scale, and cut through the clutter caused by the millions of other resumes.

Of course, everyone is in a different career situation. One person may be 28... another 68 or older, and we have different amounts of career earnings ahead of us. You might have $300,000... $1,000,000 or $2,000,000 of earnings left in your career. Or perhaps it's $3,000,000 to $10,000,000. For most people there is considerable future income at stake. That's one reason why your job search should be given priority and you should invest in your search.

Whatever your decision about how aggressively you will search, I know you will benefit from using this system. With best wishes for your success.

—Robert J. Gerberg

P.S. The editorial and design contributions to this book cannot go without mention. My special thanks to Dan McAneny in North Carolina; Paul Bokelmann in Costa Rica; Bill Oliver in New Jersey; Bob West in Texas; and Art Schill in New York. But, also to Larry Feifer in Texas; Lynette Daniels and Sue Sramek in California; Win Deal, Linda Lupatkin and Melissa Kendrick in Colorado... each of whom are independently among the leading authorities on job hunting today. The design concepts of William F. Sterling, who created the major images throughout this book, speak for themselves. So does the overall graphic design by Paula J. Berge.

This system is easy to use.
All you need to do is follow it.

Preliminary comments

On planning. Following an action plan expands your activity.

On technology. It has made job hunting a new ball game.

On changing industries. Focus on your right industry options.

On growth firms. Fast growing firms are where the action is.

On market coverage. Reach 85% of your market, not 2–3%.

On being aggressive. Would you prefer 15 bidders or just 1?

On old resumes. They no longer work in today's new market.

On contacting recruiters. Place a lot of resumes.

On contacting VCs. It can work if you have good credentials.

On creating a job. If you seek high income, this is important.

On contacting employers. Give them the right message.

On interviewing. Master chapter 16 and you'll do much better.

On negotiating. Always follow our 7-step formula.

On references. Enthusiastic people are what you want.

On being unemployed. Get into action fast.

On age concerns. For some it is when they are over 40. For most it is when they are over 50. Veteran talent is always valued, but you have to market yourself more aggressively.

On privacy issues. Because of resume scanning and job boards, exaggerations or false details can leave a forever Internet trail.

On becoming an expert at personal marketing. Job hunting is a time-to-time activity. There are very few people who won't have to do another future search. What better subject to master.

"Insanity: doing the same thing over and over again and expecting different results." —*Albert Einstein*

"We need men who can dream of things that never were." —*John F. Kennedy*

"If you think you can, you can. And if you think you can't, you're right." —*Mary Kay Ash*

Why not go after higher goals than you thought?

Even in a slow economy there are a lot more opportunities than most people think. New industries are emerging and many organizations growing. Others are making plans to grow.

1 Making sure you have the right goals

Position yourself properly for your next career move.

It may surprise you, but many people actually pursue the wrong job titles. However, if they understood their real transferable skills, they could be repositioned for different goals, and sometimes for much more advancement than they thought possible. Regardless of your most recent position, you need to think of yourself as "one of a kind" with diverse potentials.

We all have seen career fields change dramatically over a decade. Fields that once offered great opportunity have become financially confining with limited growth possibilities. Does print advertising offer the same career possibilities as it did a decade ago? Does selling in the steel industry? Does being a doctor and a general practitioner? Career fields change at a much faster pace than most people realize.

Experience has proven that if you take a narrow view of yourself, you could be making a mistake. For example, if you see yourself as a specialist (e.g., a banker), you may believe you are locked into a given career. On the other hand, you may feel you have few options because you are too much of a generalist.

More and more professionals are finding that they can have several direct careers over the course of a lifetime. Sometimes you can't see them and you stumble into them. Someone could be a radio sports broadcaster, then become an actor, then a politician... and subsequently governor of a major state and president of the United States (Ronald Reagan). And, of course, we all know many other examples, many famous and millions not so famous, but successful at many levels.

It may be that you should consider positioning yourself for more than one possible goal at this time, and running what we refer to as a "dual campaign." For example, a logical step may be seeking a new job as a VP of Marketing. But you might also have accumulated knowledge and experience that would allow you to seek a position as a General Manager, or perhaps Chief Operating Officer, or even Chief Executive Officer in the right type of organization... in the right industry.

Or you may wish to run a search for a higher paying job as a sales producer, while also exploring situations to move into a sales management role.

Many people develop careers that are specialized, but eventually make the move into general management as just mentioned. This includes executives in finance, manufacturing, operations, technology and others. One client of ours was a Director of HR who became a Vice President of HR, and then took a big jump to become Chief Administrative Officer for one of the largest consumer packaged goods firms in America. His responsibilities included overseeing all of the support functions... HR, legal, IT and IS, and so on... everything but manufacturing, marketing, finance and accounting. A former professor and university president became head of one of New York's largest museums in the world, something for which he had a passion.

Career shifts can occur at many levels. For example, a distribution specialist with UPS wanted to get into Human Resources and was successful in moving up at the same time he joined Merrill Lynch.

A project manager in the home building field saw his industry fall into decline. Faced with the prospect of declining income, he used his management skills to join Wal-Mart as an assistant store manager... with the prospect of becoming a store manager within 9 months.

So, as you review possible goals for yourself, you'll want to consider your interests, passions and experiences across a broad range, as well as your transferable skills. It may be that you should create duplicate sets of impressive resumes... each positioning you for different possible goals.

Believe it or not, the federal government tells us that there are 22,000 job titles in use today. However, 95% of all professionals fall within one of several hundred high demand career specialties.

On the pages that follow you will find a list of the 400 most popular occupations... accounting for 95% of all employment in the United States. Sales is still the number one occupation, and it is estimated that 10% of all professional and executive positions are in this field.

So, try to decide on your right career goals. And, you'll improve your chances by pursuing titles that *the market makes available in abundance.*

If you're not sure of your goals, check any fields on the following pages that might be worthwhile exploring at this time.

The 400 most popular occupations...

Where do you fit... and do any others interest you? Occupations below are listed generically... and do not necessarily refer to the level of job title you might seek... e.g., Marketing Director is listed. Your goal might be Marketing Manager, VP Marketing, Sr. VP Marketing or Chief Marketing Officer.

- Airline Pilot
- Academic Dean
- Accountant
- Account Executive
- Actor
- Actuary
- Acquisition Analyst
- Admin. Asst.
- Admin. Analyst
- Administrator

- Advertising Dir.
- Aerospace Eng'r
- Agent
- Agricult'l Inspector
- Agricult'l Scientist
- Air Traffic Cont'r
- Animal Trainer
- Anthropologist
- Appraiser
- Architect

- Art Director
- Artist
- Astronomer
- Athletic Coach
- Auditor
- Author
- Baker
- Banker
- Bankruptcy Attor'y
- Benefits Manager

- Biologist
- Bio-feedback Spec.
- Biomedical Eng'r
- Biotechnical Resch'r
- Broadcaster
- Broker
- Building Manager
- Building Contractor

- Building Inspector
- Business Analyst
- Business Planner
- Business Manager
- Buyer
- Call Center Manager
- Career Counselor
- Cash Manager
- Ceramic Eng'r
- CEO / COO / CAO

- Chef
- Chemical Dept. Spec.
- Chemical Engineer
- Chemist
- Child Care Manager
- Chief Med'l Officer
- Chiropractor
- Cinematographer
- City Housing Manager
- City Manager

- Civil Engineer
- Claims Manager
- Clinical Resch. Asst.
- Collections Manager
- Compliance Manager
- Comptroller
- Computer Manager
- Commercial Artist
- Commun. Affairs Dir.
- Communications Dir.

- Communications Eng'r
- Compensation Analyst
- Computer Programmer
- Computer Ops. Mgr.
- Computer Engineer
- Computer Operator
- Computer Graph. Spec.
- Construction Engineer

- Construction Manager
- Consultant
- Consumer Rel's Mgr.
- Contract Admin'r
- Controls Director
- Copyright Attorney
- Copywriter
- Corporate Planner
- Corrections Officer
- Cosmetologist

- Credit Analyst
- Cruise Director
- CTO / CIO
- Customer Service Mgr.
- Cryptologist
- Dancer
- Data Security Manager
- Database Manager
- Day Care Instructor
- Dentist

- Designer
- Design Engineer
- Desktop Publisher
- Developer
- Development Officer
- Diamond Merchant
- Dietitian
- Direct Marketer
- Director
- Distribution Manager

- Diversity Manager
- Economist
- EEO Compliance Mgr.
- Editor
- Education Admin'r
- Electrical Engineer
- Electro Optical Engineer
- Electronics Engineer

- Embassy Mgmt.
- Employment Agent
- Engineer Technician
- Entrepreneur
- Environ'l Analyst
- Environ'l Attorney
- Environ'l Engineer
- Environ'l Specialist
- Escrow Officer
- Estimator

- Executive Assistant
- Executive Director
- Executive Recruiter
- Facilities Manager
- Family Counselor
- Fashion Events Mgr.
- Fashion Merchandiser
- Fast Food Manager
- Film Producer
- Film Production Asst.

- Financial Analyst
- Financial Planner
- Financier
- Fine Artist
- Fish / Wildlife Spec.
- Fitness Consultant
- Flight Attendant
- Flight Engineer
- Floral Designer
- Food & Beverage Dir.

- Food Service Manager
- Forestry Technician
- Franchise Manager
- Franchise Sales
- Fraud Investigator
- Freelance Writer
- Fundraiser
- Funeral Director
- General Manager
- Geologist

- General Counsel
- Geriatric Specialist
- Gerontologist
- Glamour Photog'r
- Golf Club Manager
- Gourmet Chef
- Graphic Designer

- Groundskeeper
- Haz. Waste Mgr.
- Health Care Mgr.
- Health Therapist
- Health Svc. Admin'r
- Hearing Officer
- HMO Admin'r
- Home Economist
- Horticulturist
- Hospital Admin'r

- Hotel Manager
- HR Manager
- Importer
- Industrial Designer
- Industrial Engineer
- Information Director
- Inside Sales
- Insurance Adjuster
- Interior Decorator
- International Acct.

- Intern'l Courier
- Intern'l Lawyer
- Interpreter
- Investigator
- Investment Banker
- Investment Manager
- IT Architect
- IT Project Manager
- IT Systems Analyst
- Jeweler

- Joint Venture Mgr.
- Journalist
- Labor Negotiator
- Labor Organizer
- Labor Relations Mgr.
- Lab Services Dir.
- Lab Technician
- Land Developer
- Landscape Architect
- Law Enfor't Officer

- Lawyer
- Leasing Manager
- Legal Secretary
- Library Manager
- Litigation Attorney
- Loan Officer
- Lobbyist

- Logistics Manager
- Maintenance Mgr.
- Mgmt. Consul't
- Managed Care Dir.
- Managing Partner
- Manufacturing Dir.
- Manpower Planner
- Marine Biologist
- Market Res. Analyst
- Marketing Director

- Materials Manager
- Mathematician
- Membership Chairman
- Mechanic
- Mechanical Engineer
- Media Buyer
- Medical Investor
- Medical Secretary
- Medical Technician
- Mental Health Couns'r

- Merchandiser
- Metallographic Tech
- Metallurgical Eng'r
- Meteorologist
- Microbiologist
- MIS Manager
- Motion Picture Dir.
- Motivational Speaker
- Multimedia Director
- Musician

- Network Admin'r
- Network Specialist
- Network Operator
- New Product Mgr.
- Novelist
- Nuclear Engineer
- Nuclear Specialist
- Nutritionist
- Nursing Admin'r
- Occup. Therapist

- Oceanographer
- Office Manager
- Operations Manager
- Operations Resch. Dir.
- Optical Technician
- Optometrist
- Organiz'l Devel't Mgr.

- ☐ Outplacement Spec.
- ☐ Paralegal
- ☐ Park Ranger
- ☐ Patent Attorney
- ☐ Payroll Specialist
- ☐ Personnel Specialist
- ☐ Petroleum Engineer
- ☐ Pharmacist
- ☐ Photographer
- ☐ Physical Therapist
- ☐ Physician
- ☐ Physician Assistant
- ☐ Physicist
- ☐ Planning Director
- ☐ Podiatrist
- ☐ Political Analyst
- ☐ Political Scientist
- ☐ Politician
- ☐ Portfolio Manager
- ☐ Preschool Mgmt.
- ☐ Preschool Teacher
- ☐ Principal
- ☐ Private Banker
- ☐ Private Investigator
- ☐ Probation Officer
- ☐ Process Engineer
- ☐ Producer
- ☐ Product Manager
- ☐ Product Engineer
- ☐ Production Engineer
- ☐ Production Planner
- ☐ Professional Athlete
- ☐ Professional Coach
- ☐ Professor
- ☐ Project Engineer
- ☐ Project Manager
- ☐ Program Manager
- ☐ Property Manager
- ☐ Public Admin'r
- ☐ Public Safety Dir.
- ☐ PR Specialist
- ☐ Publisher
- ☐ Purchasing Agent
- ☐ Publishing Director
- ☐ Quality Assur'e Spec.
- ☐ Quality Con'l Eng'r
- ☐ Quality Con'l Insp'r

- ☐ Rabbi / Min'r / Priest
- ☐ Radio / TV Announcer
- ☐ Radiologic Tech
- ☐ Radiology Manager
- ☐ Railroad Engineer
- ☐ Real Estate Broker
- ☐ Recreational Director
- ☐ Recruiter
- ☐ Redevelopment Spec.
- ☐ Reg. Affairs Mgr.
- ☐ Registered Nurse
- ☐ Rehab. Counselor
- ☐ Relocation Manager
- ☐ Reporter
- ☐ R & D Manager
- ☐ Research Specialist
- ☐ Restaurant Manager
- ☐ Retail Store Manager
- ☐ Risk Analyst
- ☐ Safety Engineer
- ☐ Sales Engineer
- ☐ Sales Trainer
- ☐ Sales Promotion Mgr.
- ☐ Sales Representative
- ☐ Sales Manager
- ☐ Service Manager
- ☐ Sanitation Engineer
- ☐ Scientific Programmer
- ☐ Scientific Writer
- ☐ Securities Analyst
- ☐ Security Consultant
- ☐ Security Director
- ☐ Seminar Presenter
- ☐ Ship's Officer
- ☐ Singer
- ☐ Social Director
- ☐ Social Prog'm Planner
- ☐ Social Research
- ☐ Social Scientist
- ☐ Social Worker
- ☐ Sociologist
- ☐ Software Developer
- ☐ Software Engineer
- ☐ Soil Scientist
- ☐ Special Events Mgr.
- ☐ Special Educ. Teacher
- ☐ Special Projects Dir.

- ☐ Speech Pathologist
- ☐ Speech Writer
- ☐ Sports Event Mgr.
- ☐ Statistician
- ☐ Store Manager
- ☐ Strategic Alliance Dir.
- ☐ Strategic Plan'g Dir.
- ☐ Stress Reduc'n Spec.
- ☐ Stockbroker
- ☐ Surveyor
- ☐ Structural Engineer
- ☐ Superintendent
- ☐ Supply Chain Dir.
- ☐ System Engineer
- ☐ Systems Analyst
- ☐ Systems Programmer
- ☐ System Administrator
- ☐ Tax Specialist
- ☐ Teacher
- ☐ Tech. Support Spec.
- ☐ Technical Illustrator
- ☐ Technical Writer
- ☐ Technology Director
- ☐ Telecom Analyst
- ☐ Telesales
- ☐ Theatrical Director
- ☐ Title Examiner
- ☐ Tour Escort
- ☐ Tour Guide Director
- ☐ Traffic Manager
- ☐ Trainer Translator
- ☐ Transportation Mgr.
- ☐ Travel Agent
- ☐ Treasurer
- ☐ Tree Surgeon
- ☐ TV Programmer
- ☐ Underwriter
- ☐ Union Representative
- ☐ Univ. Administrator
- ☐ University Dean
- ☐ Urban Planner
- ☐ Vendor Rel's Director
- ☐ Veterinarian
- ☐ Viticulturist
- ☐ Warehouse Manager
- ☐ Weapons Expert
- ☐ Webmaster

Here are the most common major career changes that executives make

95% of the executives who make a major change select one of these options

- They buy a franchise or license.
- They start a new venture.
- They form a partnership.
- They invest, buy and sell.
- They purchase an existing company over time.

- They become writers... or authors.
- They buy a small firm outright.
- They become independent consultants.
- They join an existing consulting firm.
- They manage a nonprofit.

- They work in education.
- They serve on multiple boards as directors.
- They work as sales producers.
- They engage in charitable work.
- They lecture.

- They intern to learn a new field.
- They return to an earlier activity.
- They turn an avocation into a vocation.

Let's briefly review the 5 most popular changes

1.   Do you want to be a consultant?

The field has seen tremendous growth. If you decide to become a practicing consultant, your perceived professionalism will be very important. Thousands of people begin thriving consulting practices each year. Recognize that you will need some form of specialty if you are to get off to a fast start. For those attracted to consulting, remember, the knowledge you have to offer must somehow be sold. Success rests squarely on your ability to attract and keep clients. And, the biggest reason for failure is that people don't foresee the business development effort required.

If selling is not your suit, but you feel you have a great deal to offer, you will have to attract one or more partners or employees who will sell your services.

Some of the most popular consulting specialties include finance, marketing, new product development, IT and systems, executive search and outplacement, cost reduction, and public relations. There is also good activity in labor relations, engineering, design, and other technical disciplines.

If you would rather join an existing firm, there are thousands of organizations that can benefit from adding new talent. It is an easier way to get started than striking out on your own.

Regardless of the type of consulting you choose, remember that the special knowledge that makes a consultant valuable today may be obsolete in a few years. So you'll need to keep current. If you enjoy variety and intellectual challenge, consulting could be your right move.

2. Could you work as a producer?

Producers bring in business. Some examples include recruiters, financial planners, stockbrokers, real estate brokers and outplacement specialists. If you have contacts and need a shift, this role can be attractive. There are opportunities for producers in every discipline. The key is to focus on something you can do well, and that you enjoy doing.

3. Can you make an investment in some form of ownership?

It's not unusual for people to have several careers over the course of their work history.

Some executives have capital and look to find an opportunity where their efforts and capital can be joined to offer them entrepreneurial rewards.

Perhaps you have some ideas about improving a product or product line that is already being marketed. Or, you may be able to put together financing for a firm's needs. Your ability to raise capital from VCs, private investors or even friends could be critical.

These situations are most appealing when your skills complement those who are in a business with promising potential. What's more, you can pick businesses that offer you the degree of involvement that you prefer. For example, opportunities that require limited involvement might include businesses with multiple units of car washes, laundromats, theaters, apartments and parking lots.

Small chains of specialty stores can also be candidates...
e.g., pet shops, nurseries, sporting goods stores and marinas,
and product lines such as computers, men's clothing, or gourmet
foods and wines. Other possibilities include small restaurants
and inns, printing services, and small manufacturing plants.

Many existing businesses have good potential but need talent and capital to get to the next level. Associating with existing
businesses in real estate may also be suitable despite current
economic conditions... e.g., a company seeking to capitalize on
vacant land, small commercial buildings, single or multiple
family residences, abandoned factories and government repos-
sessions. Employee-investors have earned millions, but the risks
can be high.

4. Are you interested in managing a nonprofit or working in education?

Surprising to some, there are more than 20,000 trade organizations, and some are exceptionally well funded. Most trade associations are run like businesses and have similar needs.

In many respects, education is like any other service business. People must be recruited and trained, and facilities must
be operated efficiently. Information systems and data processing
are needed; funds must be raised and public relations must be
maintained. Those with corporate experience will find they are
of particular value in the graduate schools of business. In fact,
a number of universities have former corporate officers as pro-
fessors, administrators, heads of development and fundraising,
and deans of their business schools. Here, an advanced degree
is usually a prerequisite. Those who favor teaching or lecturing
may still gravitate to management.

5. What about being on a few boards?

Many executives who can bring prestige and experience to smaller
corporations become sought after for directorships. However,
it usually takes some planning. When you have served on one
board, you will likely be invited to join others.

That is particularly true if you have experience that is apparent to nominating committees. In fact, directorships on just
three or four corporations, along with committee work, can often
provide adequate income and challenge.

Some stock exchanges can direct you to clearinghouse services for executives interested in directorships. It is also possible to run a campaign aimed at existing directors, investment bankers, lawyers and CEOs by discreetly inquiring whether your services might be valuable to one or more of the companies with which they are associated. Obviously, this avenue is most feasible for executives with strong reputations. However, even if this is not the case, it is possible to develop opportunities. Think carefully about what you have to offer that would set you apart.

If you are known as an executive who can increase productivity or cut costs or if you have proven talents in securing financing, making acquisitions, or entering new markets, then it will be easy for many board members and CEOs to envision your contributions. These openings are usually coordinated by the corporate secretary, who may be a good contact. Because directorships now carry more exposure to liability, corporations no longer expect directors to serve for just a nominal sum or without proper insurance.

How important are the right goals? There is no substitute for a job you really enjoy.

There is no question that millions of men and women are settling for jobs or careers that they no longer enjoy. Nevertheless, having the right job can affect your feelings, your family, your energy and even your whole outlook on life.

Do people recognize this? Of course they do. But, when it comes to jobs and careers, most people play it safe. They tend to underestimate themselves and therefore remain in jobs that offer little future. Worse yet, many are in positions that are dull, routine and less than challenging. These people have stopped growing. They are not giving themselves a chance.

Why? Well, it's easier to stay with what is familiar rather than risk the unknown. It is also hard to overcome inertia and take that first step. However, one of the great lessons about jobs and careers is that every person has a reservoir of talents and skills that are untapped. What's more, this unused potential has been proven to exist at virtually all ages.

Interestingly, 77% of all employed professionals say that during the last year they have thought about finding a new job. Yet, most didn't really have the confidence that they could make a good move and never entered the job market.

Why do people finally try and make a move? Here are the results from a survey of more than 4,000 employed but active job seekers, people who were looking for administrative, managerial, professional or executive jobs in 2009. All had attended college. They were free to check any of the items below.

Why employed professionals think about changing jobs	Men %	Women %
Enjoy my job but wish to try something else	22	22
Blocked / need higher income*	21	39
Bored / unchallenged	19	21
Not enough enjoyment	15	17
In wrong field / industry*	15	4
Not enough responsibility	14	12
In danger of losing job	9	9
Company / industry contracting	9	9
Feel burned out	8	9
Bad political environment	8	6
Not enough independence	7	7
High pressure*	7	1
Low ego satisfaction	5	4
Not on fast track	4	6
Position was changed	4	4
Not getting along with boss	3	3
Passed over / lost out	3	3
Not in mainstream of communications*	2	11

*Factors on which there was a significant difference. This survey was composed of equal numbers of men and women. The asterisk indicates factors in which there was a significant difference. People who were seeking to relocate were not included.

"Procrastination is the thief of time."   *—Edward Young*

Think about changing your life by going for the right goals... and finding your passion.

Recapping this chapter. Surprising as it may seem, many people pursue goals that are far beneath what they really could achieve. Decide on goals that are in demand and that fit with the future you envision. Never limit your view of yourself.

Quick action steps. We use online profiles with personal discussions to surface each person's experiences, accomplishments and formal credentials. On your own, use our free profiles to surface all your marketable assets (see end of book).

"Throw yourself into some work you believe in with all your heart, live for it, die for it, and you will find happiness that you had thought could never be yours."
—Dale Carnegie (*How to Win Friends & Influence People*, 1936)

"If you have to support yourself, you had bloody well better find some way that is going to be interesting." — *Kathryn Hepburn*

"Find a need and fill it."   —*Ruth Stafford Peale*

Many people don't really sell their skills.

Most people need to identify and market 10–20 skills. If properly communicated in resumes, letters, phone discussions and interviews, they can significantly expand their appeal.

2 Selling your transferable skills

Sell your transferable skills... and you will dramatically expand your marketability.

You'll need to do more than just present your background. Don't trap yourself by thinking, *"This is simply who I am, where I've been and what I've done."* People fail because they never surface and communicate all that is marketable about themselves... and they never build their appeal beyond factual credentials.

Your starting point is to organize your lifetime of experiences and achievements. Whether you are a young attorney or a company president, there is probably much more to your story than meets the eye.

Experience has proven that many people never identify 50% of their own assets, simply because they're so close to their own situation. We've learned that most people need to identify 10 to 20 skills that, if properly communicated, can make a major difference in their career opportunities.

Each year, about 20% of the clients who come to us have settled for less, simply because they are not able to communicate their real skills. For example, one client was earning a $65,000 base after almost 20 years. Three years later, she is earning $180,000. Another executive came to us at $125,000. Three years later, he is a CEO at many times that amount. The key in both situations was to market their true assets.

It has been said time and again by psychologists, spiritual leaders and coaches that the most restrictive limits you face are those you put on yourself. So, don't put any limits on your thinking, and look at some factors that you may have overlooked... which will expand your marketability.

Your knowledge and personality are marketable

Do you have knowledge of a job, a product, a process or a market... from work, hobbies, alumni relationships, research or suppliers? If so, it may be marketable.

Personality, of course, is just a word for that combination of traits that either attracts us to someone or leaves us unimpressed. More employment decisions are based on personality and chemistry than any other factor. For example: *"He's certainly professional and quick-thinking. I like him, and better yet, I trust him. He'll fit in with our team. I need to get him into the firm."* The perception of your personality has to do with your interest and enthusiasm. How many people get hired because they showed real interest? *A lot.*

Your transferable skills are marketable

Identifying transferable skills is critical *(e.g., organizing, group presentation skills, problem solving and so on).* Employers place a premium on men and women who can move from challenge to challenge, handling assignments that draw upon skills.

Naturally, your experience can also be reviewed according to various "functions" that apply to most businesses, such as sales, production, accounting and human resources. All areas in which you have knowledge must be identified. At the same time, you need to think of your experience in terms of "action words" that describe what you did, and then translate those activities into achievements, e.g., *controlled, wrote, reshaped,* etc.

Your leadership qualities are marketable

If there is one quality you want to communicate, it is leadership ability. Experts say that leaders possess and communicate real convictions—strong feelings and principles that have grown with them over time.

Leadership is also attributed to those who create an image of operating at the leading edge… into new products, new services and new solutions. We expect our leaders to have the vision and talent to develop new things.

Another skill common to most leaders is their ability to assemble teams and motivate them to peak achievement. Often creative, intuitive and passionate, they project integrity and trust. If you have these traits, they should be marketed. Image, attitude and presence also play a role.

The importance of having a communication strategy

To appreciate a communication strategy, consider the platform of a presidential candidate. It anticipates questions on issues and formulates statements to guide the candidate's answers. Now, when any of us recruit, we have a concept in mind. In the final analysis, we hire others for the skills and abilities that certain key descriptive phrases imply.

To expand your marketability, develop stories that incorporate those phrases to create maximum interest. Without stories, most people will forget what you say in a matter of minutes. We all remember good stories. To ensure your points are memorable, we suggest a method for creating interesting stories. SOAR is an acronym that stands for Situation, Opportunities, Actions and Results. It offers a process for describing your past experience.

Our SOAR process & how it works

■ **Situations.** Describe a job by outlining the situation when you began, making it interesting.

■ **Opportunities.** Then describe opportunities the job presented. For example, "When I joined the firm, sales had been declining for three years. I saw the opportunity to target new areas."

■ **Actions.** Next, move to actions taken by you and others (the team). These actions are the most important part of the SOAR process, and a great place for the descriptive phrases.

■ **Results.** Then relate what results occurred. For the "R" in SOAR, try to quantify the results. For example, you cut costs by $100,000 or 20%. In administrative situations, you can measure results with statements like *"I did it in half the time,"* or *"The system I developed was adopted throughout the company,"* or *"I won an award."* Indicate positive things you did to help your organizations. Describe how you helped your management meet their goals, and the results they achieved. Show how you demonstrated a skill or a personal quality.

Create stories that demonstrate benefits you can bring. If you successfully managed the integration of two teams following a merger, and the new business gained market share and/or costs were reduced—by all means say so. Wherever possible, quantify with dollar amounts, percentages, etc. Even an average SOAR story is better than none at all.

Examples of SOAR stories

■ **Situation / Opportunity.** When I joined MBC Sales, the company had lost nearly $7.5 million on a new product release. I recognized an opportunity to employ my Procter & Gamble experience in marketing.

■ **Action.** With the help of the Y & R agency, I relaunched the brand, created a new television advertising campaign, and refocused all marketing efforts.

■ **Result.** Within a year, we turned an $8 million loss to a $4 million gain—30% of the firm's profits.

■ **Situation / Opportunity.** The company recruited 5,000 people a year but never had a training program.

■ **Action.** I created the firm's first training course. With a staff of 20, we introduced it in 57 markets.

■ **Result.** The firm was able to bring in recruits who produced within four weeks. In the following year, sales by newcomers accounted for $3,000,000.

200+ skills & experience factors that employers want. Which ones describe you?

If you're not sure of your skill sets and experience factors to market, review the next few pages. The more ways you describe your experience, the more you will qualify in many industries.

Skills & capabilities

- ❏ Ability to get things done quickly
- ❏ Action-oriented
- ❏ Ambitious
- ❏ Analyze situations rapidly
- ❏ Astute researcher
- ❏ Bring order out of chaos
- ❏ Bring out creativity in others
- ❏ Broad administrative skills
- ❏ Consistently find new alternatives
- ❏ Conceptual thinker
- ❏ Contacts at highest levels
- ❏ Creative
- ❏ Decisive
- ❏ Diplomatic
- ❏ Direct large meetings skillfully
- ❏ Drive "out-of-box" thinking
- ❏ Easily win people's confidence
- ❏ Effective at dealing with the public
- ❏ Effective at organizing labor
- ❏ Effective moderator and mediator
- ❏ Enterprising / dynamic
- ❏ Entrepreneurial strengths
- ❏ Excellent recruiter
- ❏ Excellent trainer
- ❏ Exceptional people skills
- ❏ Exceptional team player
- ❏ Flair for putting on events
- ❏ Genuine & sincere
- ❏ Grasp technical matters quickly
- ❏ Handle rapid change easily
- ❏ High achiever / gives 100%
- ❏ High energy / enthusiastic
- ❏ Highly articulate

Keep in mind you need to back these up with short stories

- Highly charismatic
- Highly competitive
- Highly professional
- Highly social / outgoing
- Highly organized
- In-depth technical knowledge
- Industry leader
- Innovator / imaginative
- Inspire others to top performance
- Instincts for what will sell
- Introduce change smoothly
- Intuitive decision maker
- Know international markets
- Knowledge of key markets
- Likable, friendly
- Loyal
- Make forceful group presentations
- Meet demanding objectives
- Motivator
- Natural leader
- Operations-oriented
- Perfectionist
- Perform against tight deadlines
- Persistent
- Personal contacts for new business
- Plan major conferences
- Precise thinker, logical
- Problem solver
- Proven record of success
- Public speaker
- Quick thinker
- Recognized authority in my area
- Relate easily to people at all levels
- Reliable / responsible
- Remain calm under pressure
- Resourceful
- Risk taker
- Seasoned competitor
- Self-motivated
- Sense of command
- Sense of humor
- Shirt-sleeve approach / hands-on
- Simplify complex problems
- Skilled at governmental affairs
- Skilled at union relations
- Skillful / seasoned negotiator
- Sophisticated
- Source of ideas that work
- Special visual and design taste
- Strong at consumer selling
- Strong at corporate selling
- Strong executive image / presence

- Strong group communicator
- Strong social skills
- Strong theoretical grounding
- Strong verbal communicator
- Successfully promote new ideas
- Superior sales closing skills
- Superior writing skills
- Synthesize diverse ideas
- Tactician / strategic thinker
- Troubleshooter / problem solver
- Verbally persuasive / compelling
- Versatile
- Very personable & good natured
- Very positive / upbeat
- Visionary
- Well respected
- Willing to try new approaches
- Win cooperation at all levels
- Work alone or as part of a team

Experience factors

- Achievements in international
- Acquired operations
- Aggressively managed new inventories
- Applied leading-edge technologies
- Authored major business plans
- Avoided chapter 11 filings
- Built cross-functional teams
- Built loyal teams
- Built self-sustaining teams
- Built strong marketing alliances
- Built strong technical alliances
- Chaired civic or social organizations
- Chaired multifunctional teams
- Closed millions in consumer sales
- Closed millions in corporate business
- Closed under-performing operations
- Coached winning teams
- Conceived innovative promotions
- Conducted major seminars
- Consulting firm experience
- Corporate officer level achievements
- Designed efficient systems
- Developed strategic alliances
- Developed new systems
- Directed diversification
- Directed startup
- Division officer level achievements
- Enhanced corporate image
- Entrepreneurial experience

❏ Established new standards
❏ Experience with market leader
❏ Experienced at change management
❏ Experienced at cost control
❏ Experienced in growth firms
❏ Experienced with regulatory agencies
❏ Formulated top policies
❏ Fortune 1000 experience
❏ Handled strategic planning
❏ Have had P&L responsibility
❏ Helped clients grow revenues
❏ High-tech experience
❏ Implemented sweeping changes
❏ Improved customer relations
❏ Improved productivity
❏ Improved sales / profits
❏ Increased shareholder value
❏ Installed superior controls
❏ Integrated new technologies
❏ Joint venture experience
❏ Large material responsibilities
❏ Led major expansion
❏ Long-range planning experience
❏ Made go / no-go decisions
❏ Managed a large downsizing
❏ Managed a lot of people
❏ Managed a successful operation
❏ Managed complex operations
❏ Managed large budgets
❏ Managed large investment portfolios
❏ Managed rapid growth
❏ Managed succession planning
❏ Manufacturing experience
❏ Minimized liability exposure
❏ Minimized litigation
❏ Modernized manufacturing
❏ Multi-plant experience
❏ Multi-product / multi-market exper.
❏ Large company experience
❏ Negotiated foreign contracts
❏ Negotiated mergers or acquisitions
❏ Negotiated major deals
❏ Nonprofit experience
❏ Opened new markets
❏ Opened new plants

❏ Orchestrated major change
❏ Overhauled ineffective methods
❏ Overhauled vendor relationships
❏ Participated in a breakthrough
❏ Patent / invention holder
❏ Planned fundraising programs
❏ Private company experience
❏ Procured major funds, grants
❏ Project management experience
❏ Public company experience
❏ Published author of articles
❏ Published author of books
❏ Recapitalized organization
❏ Recovered tax payments
❏ Recruited top performers
❏ Recruited substantial volunteers
❏ Re-engineered processes
❏ Reorganized and revitalized
❏ Restructured debt
❏ Revamped operations
❏ Revamped supply chain
❏ Salvaged unprofitable operations
❏ Served on civic boards
❏ Served on corporate boards
❏ Served on key committees
❏ Served on nonprofit boards
❏ Service firm experience
❏ Skilled at crisis management
❏ Skilled at outsourcing
❏ Sold off undesirable properties
❏ Started prototype operations
❏ Streamlined processes
❏ Substantial line experience
❏ Substantial staff experience
❏ Substantial startup experience
❏ Succeeded in declining market
❏ Succeeded where others failed
❏ Ten+ years experience
❏ Top management experience
❏ Turned around operations
❏ Twenty+ years experience
❏ Upgraded investor relations
❏ Work a 60+ hour week
❏ Worked closely with top mgmt.

To expand your marketability, you have to sell what employers are buying. They think in terms of phrases that people associate with solving problems or capitalizing on opportunities. Key phrases should be communicated in all your resumes and letters… and in all phone discussions and interviews. This will expand your marketability beyond your factual credentials.

When you start selling skills... people will start calling. It builds your appeal.

Recapping this chapter. Many people market less than 50% of their skills. Chances are you have 10 to 20 skills that can dramatically expand your marketability.

Quick action steps. Use our free marketability profile *(see end of book)* with hundreds of "in-demand" skills to check. On your own, if you prefer, you can also list the skills you've used and delete those that could not be used in another industry. For each achievement, note the challenges faced and results achieved.

"If you board the wrong train, it's no use running along the corridor in the other direction." —*Dietrich Bonhoeffer*

Why you need to be in the right industry

The right industry	The wrong industry
Pay increases	Fewer raises
Promotions	Slower promotions
Stock options	Possible cutbacks
Good environment	Reduced pay
Long-term career	Forced retirement

Careers can be made... or broken... by your industry.

You can't compare the future of the airline industry, steel or textiles... with industries like the Internet, nutrition, renewable energy... or many other growth industries.

3 Uncovering your industry options

Pursue the right new industry options and you may change your life.

People should be prepared to market themselves so that they are attractive to employers across a broad range. The reality is that people of all ages are moving into exciting new industries.

Transition to a new industry is easier than it used to be. Historically, people have overrated the barriers and underrated their abilities to move into new areas. The vast majority of all new jobs are created by small and mid-sized businesses. So, while major employers are still important, you may want to explore positions with startups or emerging companies.

If you choose the right industry, you will have more growth opportunities, perhaps meaningful stock options, an environment that is likely to be more positive, a chance for more regular pay increases and probably advancement.

> **"** 87% of all job seekers start out with the thought of restricting themselves to industries where they have past experience. But it doesn't have to be this way. **"**

Identifying new industry options

The first way to do this is to read and increase your awareness of the fastest growing industries and companies. These firms have to go outside their industry to find the best talent and skills.

The second way is to list characteristics of your industries… and find similar industries. We use software to compare your industry's characteristics with 2,500 others… e.g., 35 industries may be an 85% match.

Keep in mind that projecting some form of an "industry hook" is the next best thing to having industry experience. Group your possibilities three ways: (1) close industry hooks, easy possibilities; (2) medium industry hooks, next best; (3) far reach or stretch industry hooks.

When changing industries, you also don't want to overlook your leverage power... the added benefits you may bring by virtue of your contacts or knowledge. You may be able to bring a team with you that helped in similar situations.

Despite our recent economic slowdown, new companies have sprung up throughout America. Established organizations are reexamining the way they do business. Medium-sized companies are expanding. New industries exist that are employing tens of thousands.

The more you appear to know about an industry, the easier it is to generate interviews. Virtually all employers look for "common ground" when hiring a new person. For example, do you have experience in or knowledge of similar product lines, distribution channels, manufacturing methods or problems in their industry? There can be other similarities. Consider the scope of operations, the role of advertising and promotion, the importance of the sales organization, the influence of labor, and other items.

Naturally, the harder it is to demonstrate knowledge of an industry, the less likely an executive is to make a move into it. That rule applies to all major disciplines: sales, marketing, finance, manufacturing and operations. It is less important in staff disciplines. Here are some examples of commonplace changes:

■ A marketing executive with a tobacco company joined a cosmetics firm. Why? Their methods of marketing are similar.

■ The EVP of a circuit board company was recruited to become president of a firm that makes power packs. Why? These industries have similarities in manufacturing and sales, even though the products are so different.

■ An executive of an aerospace company was recruited to become chairman of a small company that sells high tech services to defense contractors. Why? The key was the new chairman's contacts and knowledge of the marketplace.

Here are a few growth industries that have positive futures. There are a great many more.

Cosmetic surgery
Smart phones
Green tech
Specialty wines
Digital SLRs

Computer security
Fashion watches
Digital book readers
Nuclear power
Health (natural) foods

Clean coal technology
Anti-aging drugs
Pollution monitoring
Medical equipment
Retirement planning

Virtual marketing
Robotics
Solar cell operations
Personal security
Specialty firearms

Home health care
Encryption
Optics technology / laser
Assisted living
Outpatient services

Touch screen technology
Organic foods
Medical records automation
Digital banking software
LED televisions

Computer animation
Artificial limbs
Paper thin speakers
Sonar sensors
Pathogen detectors

Solid ink technology
Facial recognition services
Flat screen TVs
Wireless communications
Online auctions

Personal marketing services
Skin care products
Physical fitness
Teleconferencing
Nutrition

Hospital efficiency
Corporate security
Electronic security
Microbiological agents
Immune system drugs

Body care products
Micro finance programs
Online gaming
Specialty shipbuilding
Online entertainment

Psycho pharmacology
Algae farms
Luxury theaters
Home remodeling
Technical trade schools

Electronic storage devices
Light intensity control
Soy based food products...
and many others.

Solar powered cell phones
Sleep apnea therapy
Real time language translation
Smart pens
ATM processors

■ The controller of a component manufacturer was brought in as president of a company that produces plastic packaging. Why? The similarities have to do with cost control as the #1 challenge.

If you have no knowledge of an industry but have an interest in exploring situations, extra steps are recommended. As mentioned, the easiest way to acquire knowledge of a new industry, and gain credibility for it, is to read trade publications. They will bring you up to date on personnel changes, new products, information on companies, and challenges as seen by industry leaders.

Another way to acquire knowledge is to talk with executives already in the field. In some cases you can go further by getting more formal input, attending trade shows and the like. The most radical approach is to take a lower level job in an industry in order to acquire knowledge.

During the last decade we've witnessed declines in many industries. However, don't overlook opportunities in troubled industries. Executives who have worked for firms under pressure often find they can be valuable to distributors or consulting firms. Those who learned tough lessons in competitive battles can function as veterans in any industry.

As you begin to consider industry options, you'll also need to decide whether you should take a narrow view. This is essential if there are a lot of growth companies in the industries to which you relate best.

However, if you are part of an industry that is suffering a decline, then you will want to adopt a broad view of your options. The more you understand the dynamics of a market, the more you can spot potential opportunities.

Historically, executives tend to overrate the barriers and to underrate their own abilities to make contributions in new areas. It is, of course, up to you to take the initiative to learn something about new companies, new industries, and the problems and opportunities they face.

As you review potential industries of interest, remember that while glamorous high tech and service businesses receive 90% of the publicity today, many executives will find far more opportunities in industries that are considered low tech or non-glamorous by today's standards.

Why not pursue jobs in many industries? Growth industries are where the excitement is.

Recapping this chapter. Be prepared to market yourself so that you are attractive across a broad range of industries. When you identify your industry options and market your skills, you will expand your market by 500% or more.

Quick action steps. Through our Job Market Access Center, our software helps identify industry options. But on your own, enter "growth industries" in a search engine and visit selected sites. Then visit sites with SIC or NAICS codes, and use the Internet or directories to find firms in preferred industries and areas.

"On the human chess board, all moves are possible."
—Miriam Schiff

It's absolutely critical to minimize liabilities.

There are over 25 common liabilities that can cause you to be ruled out—and ways for handling each of them.

4 Neutralizing your liabilities

Minimize the impact of your negative liabilities.

Every recruiter looks for liabilities. At the same time, the best recruiters know that there is no perfect candidate. But, how you handle liabilities is key. Listed below are the results of a survey of 2,500 professionals who were still in the job market *after 12 months*. This reflects what they felt were their problems.

Search issues they blamed
96%+ Lacked access to right openings
91%+ Needed better resume
87%+ Lacked industry options
77%+ Failed in interviews

Liability issues they blamed
68%+ Unemployment hurt
65%+ Age was a problem
62%+ Too specialized
55%+ Experience in a single industry
47%+ Lacked blue chip experience
29%+ Changed jobs too often
22%+ Titles lacked career progression
20%+ Previous firm performed poorly
20%+ Reference issues
16%+ Left short-term job
15%+ Recent jobs were too similar
13%+ Had shifted from main field
9%+ Was seen as overqualified

Liability issues can haunt you. If you plan how you will neutralize them, you will get much better results. Any good marketer, whether it's IBM or Apple... knows their products aren't perfect, but they find ways to market them and overcome any shortcomings.

If you have an "age" liability, here's some advice.

It is always interesting to listen to the opinions of people about age barriers and job hunting. Depending on their age, beliefs and other factors, you will hear a lot of different opinions.

It is true that in job seeking, "being too old" is often a negative. It is also true, however, that many people stay in dead-end jobs because they believe they are too old to change jobs. It doesn't have to be that way.

At whatever age you begin to feel you have a liability, winning a new job is seldom a simple task. You could have just hit 40 in the advertising business... or lost your executive job at 63.

However, despite any difficulties in adjustment that may be required, a good job change can bring you a totally new feeling about life.

It is always amazing to see what the excitement of new work, a new location, and new associates does for people... in mental stimulation and good feelings. It can make you look and act ten years younger.

Here's your reality. Age becomes a major problem only at that point when you mentally accept it as an obstacle. But, there are many things you can do to offset the imagined and real problems associated with age, starting with an examination of your own beliefs and attitudes.

Having the right mindset

If you are feeling uncomfortable about your work situation, but not doing anything about it, first ask yourself... *are you using age as a convenient excuse?*

Many people who either do not have the confidence... don't know how to search for a job... or aren't willing to go through the work, will use age as an excuse. If this is you, you need to address it honestly, so you can begin to take action.

There are several things you need to write down and remind yourself of daily. Consider the following: At this moment you possess all the skills, know-how and personal strengths that enabled you to make significant contributions to employers over the years. They can still be applied today to help literally tens of thousands of employers.

So the question is not whether you should seek a new job, or seek a job if you are unemployed. It is what you should say and how you should say it, so that you get your *"selling proposition"* across to as many suitable employers as possible. The goal is simple. Have at least one person in one company make the decision to hire you for a position you would enjoy.

The most common liabilities

Few professionals devote enough thought to properly handling their liabilities... in their resumes and letters... and in their phone conversations and interviews.

❏ I'm currently unemployed.
❏ I've been unemployed for a while.
❏ My age could be a concern.
❏ I've changed jobs too often.
❏ I may be too specialized.

❏ I may be too generalized.
❏ I've been too long with one firm.
❏ I've been too long in one industry.
❏ I lack a degree.
❏ My career may have peaked.

❏ I lack large company experience.
❏ My firm has done poorly.
❏ My jobs have all been similar.
❏ I lack career progression.
❏ My employment history has gaps.

❏ I've been passed over.
❏ My references are doubtful.
❏ I haven't been a leader.
❏ I've been an entrepreneur.
❏ I have a short work history.

❏ I need to change careers.
❏ I've just changed positions.
❏ My achievements are minor.
❏ My earnings have been low.
❏ Achievements aren't measurable.

❏ I need confidentiality.
❏ No experience in an employer's industry.
❏ High earnings may disqualify me.
❏ My job titles aren't impressive.
❏ I don't have any line experience.
❏ I need much more income.

Based on our surveys, over 95% of all professionals and executives start their job search without really figuring out how to handle their liabilities. You don't want to make the same mistake.

The importance of new industry options for people with age concerns

Today there are many dozens of either young or vibrant industries. And, in these industries there are thousands of recently formed companies with young management, and their emphasis is definitely on youth.

Despite that, you are likely to find most of them have at least two or three senior professionals who are highly valued.

Don't forget that several studies have shown senior employees to be more reliable. Many are just as quick to pick up new information as other age groups.

Young management teams often realize that they need to be balanced with the wisdom that extra experience brings, and will prefer an older candidate for functions such as legal, finance and administration.

Another daily reminder should be to review your beliefs and attitudes. Here is a well known fact among psychologists who study such things. *We are limited or not limited* according to our beliefs about ourselves and what is possible for us, and that generally we are treated by others in accord with our expectations—*about how they will treat us.*

Because we tend to get what we expect, and because people tend to reflect back to us the beliefs and attitudes we are projecting, you need to examine your beliefs about yourself and about what's possible "career wise" at this stage.

If your beliefs are limiting or negative, start working on them. Recognize that all of us filter reality through our attitudes and beliefs, so what we perceive doesn't necessarily reflect reality, but just the way we are seeing it at the moment.

If you have held some limiting beliefs related to age, it's very likely that your "filter" has been distorted toward the negative, and has been reinforced by many of those around you. So, consider writing down your beliefs in this area, not as fact, but as beliefs. *Start each one with the words, "I believe."*

If any of them are negative or limiting, then write a corresponding positive version. As you may know, any belief can be justified by the facts, depending upon which facts you focus upon. Use "selective perception" to focus on and write down all the events that support the positive beliefs and ignore any negative ones.

If the daily media are full of only negative news, don't read it... read only positive literature, listen to music that makes you feel good... engage in physical activity that energizes you.

Visualize yourself being warmly greeted by interested prospective employers, and make corresponding verbal affirmations. It's not new to anyone that visualization has proven effective in many fields, including sports and medicine, and there is no reason to doubt that it also works when we have to sell ourselves into a new job.

These activities will help you see the world in a brighter light. You will gradually develop more positive expectations about what's possible for you and how people will react to you.

In recent years you may have been subconsciously projecting to the world that you feel you're too old for any really good job opportunities, so make this the time to start changing that message and bring into focus the good times. Working on building positive beliefs and expectations is one way to do it.

What to reveal... when you have an age concern

Never mention your age in your resume and don't include every bit of experience you've ever had. Choose to leave out earlier experience altogether, or simply summarize years of earlier experience under the heading, "previous." As a general rule, emphasize only the last 10 years and your achievements during that time. Never include the year of graduation from college or when you received an advanced degree. If any of your leisure activities require physical exertion, mention them.

When age is a concern... use more letters and emails

You may wish to use email or letters for your initial contact with employers. They can be more easily structured to selectively cover dates, length of experience and other factors, so that your age is not apparent. In all correspondence, and in interviews, emphasize those characteristics that represent the best of both youth and experience. It will be to your advantage to highlight your sound business judgment and solid record of achievement, as well as your versatility and adaptability, a high energy level, and proven capacity for delivering results in a fast-paced, demanding environment.

In interviews your maturity will be obvious. Point out that you bring the experience and judgment of a seasoned performer, combined with the enthusiasm and energy level of a person who is excited about his or her job, and who expects to make significant contributions.

It will be to your advantage to direct the interview to a discussion of the functional areas where they need help.

Ask questions that direct the discussion toward the functions and personal strengths that will be most important for the person who wins the job, and when they are identified, relate examples of how you have used those precise abilities and strengths to make significant contributions to your employer.

The most memorable and credible way to do that is through concise SOAR stories that show how you analyzed situations well, took appropriate actions, and achieved measurable results. The actions in particular should show that you have an energetic, aggressive approach to getting things done, as well as know-how and knowledge in the areas most important for the job.

Remember, project self-confidence, high energy, enthusiasm and positive expectations. If you do, you are likely to be treated and responded to accordingly.

Actions to take in your search

As you become older, at any age your need to make a good impression becomes even more vital. If you're not in good physical condition, consult with a doctor and start a regular program of exercising.

Or, consult with health and beauty professionals to make sure your appearance is at its best. Avoid dated clothing, and invest in higher quality, tailored clothing appropriate for the level of position and income you are seeking.

When choosing the types of positions and industries you are targeting, give a lot of thought to how closely you can match your strengths and achievements to those that are likely to be required for those positions.

Ask yourself, *"If I were doing the hiring for that position, why would I hire someone with my background?"*

Examine your past contributions closely, and take sufficient time to prepare and rehearse several action-oriented stories that demonstrate your talent for moving rapidly to get results in the types of situations that resemble those likely to be faced by the person who wins the job you are seeking.

Look for as many specific result indications as possible. Be prepared to give a wealth of evidence using memorable stories. They will reassure the prospective employer that, from your perspective, age is not a factor, and you are more than ready to dig into challenging problems and opportunities. Develop and coach enthusiastic references from selected individuals you can trust inside your employer organization, if possible.

Also make use of references from outside, e.g., customers, suppliers, sales reps, consultants, etc., who will be happy to attest to your high energy level, action orientation, ambition, and ability to deliver results in a demanding, fast-paced environment.

Review your resume with these references, and make sure they keep a copy available to scan when and if they are called. *Make it easy for them to send people a link to your personal marketing website (see chapter 6).*

Your search when you have an age concern

In certain industries, some people start getting concerned about their job search when they are over 40. But, when they are over 50 the reality of their age really becomes an issue for most.

There is no question that in many organizations you will encounter a bias that takes away what might have been opportunities for you. To compensate for the realities of the marketplace, you need to run a broader and more aggressive search... and allow for higher rates of rejection that are simply part of the job market experience when you are older.

The channels available to you for running your search won't be as broad as others. For example, don't spend much effort on recruiters, because your response will be too low for the time and expense you put into contacting them.

The same will be true when you answer published openings in newspapers, magazines or online. The one exception is if you are highly specialized. Occasionally, companies will put out searches for specialists without a concern about age.

Marketing yourself to targeted employers is a channel on which you will need to focus. Again, you will need to double or even triple the numbers of someone without an age concern... but you will find your way to people who simply want results.

Recapping truth, fiction and the age barrier

As firms have been re-engineered, many people in their 50s and early 60s have had their jobs eliminated. A look at *PepsiCo, Inc.* gives a good example of the trend. Data on the firm indicates 36 officers had a median age of 47.

When we encounter situations where age is a problem, we compensate by developing a more aggressive action plan. The reality is that today, more employers than ever prefer young professionals... often because it costs less.

At the same time there is another reality. Many people in their late 50s are connecting with fast-growing companies in new industries where experience is in demand. Last year, we also successfully helped clients in their 60s and early 70s. Success depended on each person's background, but the starting point for you is to avoid putting limits on your thinking. Just for the record, a common thread bound the following people. Each made their major accomplishments after they became "senior citizens."

Sir Isaac Newton, Louis Pasteur, Cocoa Chanel, Mother Theresa, Margaret Thatcher, Socrates, Thomas Jefferson, Adolf Zuckor, George Burns, Kirk Krekorian, Madeleine Albright, Galileo, Talleyrand, Grandma Moses, Armand Hammer, Katheryn Graham, John McCain, Voltaire, Commodore Vanderbilt, Winston Churchill, Benjamin Spock and Ronald Regan.

"Age is a question of mind over matter. If you don't mind, it doesn't matter."   —Satchel Paige

Minimize any negative information. Failure to neutralize liabilities is not a winning strategy.

Recapping this chapter. Everyone looks for your liabilities. You can be talented, but if you can't neutralize perceptions about your liabilities, you will be at risk. There are over 25 common liabilities, and solutions exist for handling each one.

Quick action steps. On our Job Market Access Center we provide solutions for all liabilities. But you can use this book's list and master the ARTS process in chapter 16. For any liability that might prompt someone to raise a concern, decide how you'd "redirect" to the positive qualities being sought. Develop SOAR stories for each answer. And, get liabilities out of your resume.

"It is extraordinary how extraordinary the ordinary person is."
—George Will

Traditional or "old style" resumes no longer work.

With 30 million resumes in circulation … and the Internet so dominant as a recruiting tool… you must alter your approach.

5 Making sure you have superior resumes

Using multiple resumes can bring you much greater response.

This chapter could by itself significantly alter the results of your job search. Here's why I say this. Over the last 10 years we've learned what really works and what doesn't. In this discussion I will share this with you.

To appreciate the importance of superior resumes, let's first talk a little bit about the competition, and why it has devastated so many talented people. And keep in mind that when you look for a new job, you are reduced to how you look on paper.

Today, the number of resumes in circulation exceeds the imagination. GE receives 800,000 resumes a year... but they only hire about 4,000 people. That's 1 out of every 200. Other well-known firms say they get over 1,000 resumes for every opening. And, when it comes to submitting your resume to an attractive ad... you should know that employers are now getting hundreds of candidates. Leading recruiters, like Korn Ferry and Heidrick and Struggles, now claim to receive more than 1,500 resumes a work day... 30,000 each month.

Unfortunately, despite the enormous competition, many people create a resume, show it to some friends or family members and then assume it's fine. Ann Landers is famous for many quotes, but one applies here. *"Don't accept your dog's admiration as conclusive evidence that you are wonderful."*

Just how good is your resume?

While many professionals still use traditional resumes, with this amount of competition, the fact is they don't work very well anymore. The reason is that most of these resumes have one or more of the six major resume weaknesses... that can restrict job hunting success. So, let's start by having you assess your current resume... to see if it has these weaknesses.

1—Does your resume look like others? Your resume must start by projecting an outstanding image... one that sets you apart. It must be eye-catching... not ordinary, plain vanilla and flat.

2—Does your resume reveal liabilities? Even top executives can find themselves continually derailed... because of the negative information they made available... without realizing it.

3—Third, does your resume sell transferable skills? Or, does it just sell your history and experience? Selling skills is an absolute necessity if you want to expand your market... change industries... join a growth firm... appeal to venture capitalists... or impress CEOs and other key decision makers.

4—Does your resume show how you can contribute? Or does it, like millions of others, force the reader to try to figure out how to use you? If so, you won't get many calls. Why? Because people simply won't take the time to study resumes. They'll put it in the "no pile"... or toss it. Your resume has just 20 seconds to make your case... and get people to read further... or better yet... call you. If it doesn't do this, you won't even get in the game.

5—Is your resume scanning ready? Scanning software has forever changed the selection process. Most organizations only keep the best 5% of resumes they receive... and scan just the first page into their databases. When employers are looking for someone, they simply input key words... bring up matching resumes... and review them. That determines who gets interviewed.

6—Is your resume dynamic and a strong selling document? In today's market, you must inspire the reader... being boring doesn't work. The words you select need to have some reasonable punch, substance and sparkle. Your resume needs to be interesting and compelling. There are a lot of excellent competitors out there... and the worst thing you can do is undersell yourself.

So how does your resume stack up?
Is it superior... good... or just average?

Our recommended approach

After analyzing every resume style... we developed a new approach—one where people are equipped with three different styles of superior resumes... materials that meet all of the concerns we've mentioned. Why does having several resumes give you a major advantage? The answer is... that each one is targeted for a different application... and each is what we call an "A" resume. When you have an "A" resume, it's not likely to be just two times more effective than a "B" resume—it's more likely to be 20 to 25 times more effective. Plus... you have the advantage of having more tailored materials for the three most common situations where you will be submitting resumes.

When we prepare an introductory resume... for people to get the very best results, we also always follow seven key rules:

- **The resume must be one page**
- **Preferred jobs must be listed first**
- **The top third must be a summary**
- **Liabilities must be neutralized**
- **Transferable skills must be sold**
- **A first-class image must be presented**
- **Resumes must be scanning-ready with relevant key words**

Keep in mind that a good resume has to cover the past, but it is really all about your future. So now let's look at the three different resumes you should have available before you begin your search.

A universal resume

The most essential is a universal resume—a one-page document that will be your introductory resume. Most people mistakenly believe that they need to tell their whole story in their initial resume. The reality is that you get better results when your initial resume is interesting, with a feeling of action—but short. This resume must be suitable for key word scanning, have short paragraphs, and be compelling. It must be headlined by a job title listing (e.g., Director of Marketing) that an employer might have available. Remember, your resume is an ad... *not an epitaph.*

Our research staff randomly selected
1,000 resumes, and we found that less
than 20% made the type of position
and level they were seeking... immediately apparent.

An "Internet (or electronic)" resume

This second resume needs to be shorter and to the point... usually no more than two-thirds of one page. It is surprising how few devote any thought to the way their resumes appear at the receiving end of an email transmission. When you are online, less is more. All you want is a positive response.

A "quick-response" resume

This third resume makes it easy for you to respond quickly to emerging situations you read about. It positions the text on the right-hand side of the page so you can write handwritten notes and dispatch a resume without a cover letter. Clients consistently tell us that executives respond well to their notes, which cited events that were signals of emerging jobs.

Other guidelines

■ Highly marketable achievers should have a resume that sets them apart from average performers, convincingly.

■ Anyone unemployed should have a resume that emphasizes achievements over dates... shows momentum, how they made contributions... and why they can be a key solution.

■ Those whose achievements are less than stellar... need to show how they can contribute in specific ways, in a dramatic manner, while emphasizing personal factors and transferable skills.

■ Those whose employers have not fared well... despite their individual contributions... need to tell compelling stories that will separate their value from the fortunes of their employer.

■ Those with a checkered career, or too many jobs, or who have age concerns... need to find a way to minimize liabilities... while emphasizing selected positives.

■ Can some people use more than three resumes? Yes. Leave-behind resumes... after you have been interviewed... should be longer and more revealing.

An "interview" resume

An interview resume is 2 to 3 pages. It is for presentation during or after interviews when employers want to know more and reveals more about you. If you have an executive biography, you would not need this resume.

**Your resumes define your "personal brand"...
they must differentiate you from the competition.**

5 An executive biography

An executive biography is a 3 to 5 page narrative document, written in a third-person style. It uses interesting stories, rich in detail, and is favored by top recruiters and senior executives. **Today, these are the "Mercedes of presentations."** Those seeking $150,000 to 1 million dollars+ should have one.

Decision makers often forward resumes to others to get consensus. And sometimes, you never meet the top people, but nevertheless they will often review your resume. The offer depends on a "thumbs up" from the resume presentation.

A "biography" communicates a total feeling about you and your skills. And, it should also say that you are interesting...that you can do certain things extremely well... that you have excellent personal qualities. To prepare a biography, be patient enough to do many drafts. When your final biography hits the marketplace, it *can easily have 300% to 500% more impact* than something else you might have turned out.

❝Top recruiters... people who get assignments to fill the most prestigious jobs in America... rewrite resumes before showing them to their corporate clients. 3 to 5 page executive biographies are what they create.❞

Customized marketing letters

Certain people who must avoid revealing liabilities should use personalized letters, but they need to be focused and motivating. Custom letters, tailored to the needs of organizations, can be highly effective. The letters people may require can include the following 12 letters for different occasions:

- For responding to openings
- For contacting recruiters
- For contacting venture capitalists
- For responding to emerging jobs
- For direct contact with employers
- For third-party letters to employers
- For contacting directors of associations
- For networking associates and friends
- For networking alumni
- For networking influential people
- For setting up potential references
- For following up your interviews

Cover letters should be interesting and brief. The key rule here is to get to the point and make sure it's good. **Letter resumes** are stand-alone letters that you will forward without a resume. They are valuable when you want to tailor the description of your credentials and avoid revealing any liabilities. They are always recommended for people who wish to change careers or industries. *Remember, the letters are advertisements for you.*

Handwritten memos are fast and easy to send off, plus executives are used to them. If your resume is on target for your audience, attaching such notes can work very well. Notes that emphasize what you can do, as well as the results you can bring, are ideal.

Before writing your letters, have a clear picture of what you want to say. **The opening** should demonstrate interest (knowledge of the firm, its industry, etc.) and explain why you are writing. **The body** should deal with your best selling points and convey benefits. **The closing** should restate interest, confirm your desire for an interview, and say when you will follow up. Keep it simple. Letters are skimmed, not analyzed.

Your resumes and the important "preselling" role

People face immense competition at every stage of their search. This competition will not only affect your ability to get your credentials viewed... but when you are invited for an interview, there are likely to be five to ten other qualified people under consideration.

So, your resumes need to be written with an eye toward reducing interview pressure... by preselling you. The ideal reaction when you meet someone should be *"Paul, I was really looking forward to meeting you. I have the feeling you can really help."*

"Promise, large promise, is the soul of an advertisement."
—*Samuel Johnson*

20 letter writing commandments

1 Use the name of the person or firm in body of the letter.

2 Letters are warmer if you use pronouns like "I" or "we."

3 Good letters are fast moving. They read like you speak.

4 Always be enthusiastic.

5 If you have related industry experience, mention it early.

6 Communicate potential benefits.

7 Use short sentences, preferably 3 to 4 line paragraphs.

8 Don't oversell. "If this guy is so good, why the hard sell?"

9 Never begin a letter by asking for a job.

10 When answering ads, tailor responses to requirements.

11 When possible, offer to share some beneficial "ideas."

12 Avoid income or why you are looking.

13 Use action words and brief descriptions.

14 Sign letters with your full name.

15 Read them out loud and then edit them.

16 Commit yourself to a follow-up.

17 When writing to employers who have been undergoing change, relate your experience to their opportunities.

18 With an influential person, recognize their position in a complimentary manner and be brief.

19 Third party letters can be powerful and act as a strong endorsement. Make it easy for the third party to assist.

20 Follow-up letters must show continued enthusiasm.

What people say about these resumes

■   *"Adjectives would not adequately convey my admiration for the biography concept."*

■   *"You are clearly into what works, and seem to be years ahead. Your three recommended resumes. All played their role."*

■   *" I realize now that I never really told my story properly. My resumes were the key to my success."*

■   *"I had a string of short-term experiences. The materials I used handled them, and compensated for my age concerns."*

■   *"Your three-resume approach was the key for me. I won't say they made my campaign a slam dunk, but it worked. "*

■   *"Your resumes were the primary drivers in helping me produce a stream of calls."*

30 million resumes are in circulation. Is that competition... or what?

Recapping this chapter. Northrop Grumman's technology division receives over 720,000 resumes a year... for about 3,600 openings. IBM, Intel and Microsoft get more than 1,000 resumes for every opening. In this market, it's simply not enough to have an average resume. We've found that a three-resume approach will optimize your success. When you use this concept and distribute enough materials, you will lift your response several times over.

Quick action steps. We write all resumes for our clients. On your own, restructure your resume to follow the same rules our staff uses. Then, create a 2/3 page electronic resume to be used on the Internet. Last, create a version where the left margin is wide enough to permit a handwritten note. Check all versions against our criteria. For letters, follow our "20 commandments."

"The only sin is mediocrity."   *—Martha Graham*

Personal marketing websites can speed your search.

Less than 1 in 100 job seekers develop a personal marketing website. However, it can make job hunting easier and faster.

6 Setting up your personal marketing website

Take advantage of a personal marketing website... and drive people to it.

Job hunting is all about getting enough of the "right people" to look at your credentials. A "Personal Marketing Website"... *PMW for short*, is a website that presents your universal resume... and sometimes your biography... for those who wish to review it.

What information should it contain?

When your PMW site opens, it should bring up a summary. It should enable interested parties to view a brief summary about you... one that can be read in 20 to 30 seconds. Your name and contact information should be at the top. Then the position (or positions) for which you are best qualified should be highlighted. After that you want a subset of key words that represent experience factors or skills that people normally want with the position you are seeking.

The remaining information in your summary should be the most marketable information about you. In terms of length, your full summary should be equivalent to about one-third of a normal 8-1/2 x 11" page. Besides a summary, you want a second menu button for people to click to read a brief listing of your work experience and titles held. Other menu selections should also allow people to click to your education separately, as well as your full resume, and a button for download.

Create your personal marketing website in HTML... not in "Flash." Don't go wild and overdo your presentation. It may be impressive, but it will look as if you are trying too hard. Also, including a photograph may be good if you are in a special situation, or perhaps in the broader entertainment industry, but it is usually not the approach that's best for most people.

Here's how this works at our firm. When we write resumes, we create a distinctive and professional "Personal Marketing Website." Displaying one on the web in color... is an impressive way of presenting yourself. It gives you a fast, no-cost way to get your presentation in front of the right decision makers.

How? Because you can simply send out emails with a link to your "Personal Marketing Website." All you need to do is get the names of decision makers… and emails of key employers… throughout the U.S.… or the world… in industries that are right for you… or in the area where you want to live.

Can this make networking easier?

Yes. For people you already know… all you do is send an email to let them know that you are open to new opportunities… and that you put up a new and unique "personal marketing website." And, when people see your presentation, they will be far more impressed than anything you could say over the phone.

For those with access to our Job Market Access Center (JMAC), you can even comfortably network *people you don't know*. For example, you can quickly get the names of alumni from your school who hold influential jobs… or others who worked with you some years ago… or executives in an industry or metro area… whose advice and referrals you'd appreciate.

Can a PMW also be used for responding to ads?

Absolutely. Mention your link in a compelling email and you'll have a surefire way to dramatically stand out from everyone else who answers an ad. The bottom line is that if you're in the market today… and don't have a "Personal Marketing Website"… you will be searching with an unnecessary competitive disadvantage.

What some people did with their personal marketing website

■ *"I have an MBA from Columbia University. I sent an email to 400 influential graduates of Columbia, here in New York. It was all I needed."*

■ *"I got the names and corporate emails of the top 100 ad agencies in England and sent an email with a link to all of them. 11 interviews resulted."*

■ *"I sent links to everyone on my LinkedIn site and asked them to forward it to anyone who might be interested."*

Your personal marketing website is your power presentation.

Recapping this chapter. This makes it easy for people to view your credentials... and especially your transferable skills. It won't be long before these websites are used by almost everyone. They can enable you to get far greater worldwide market exposure... in much less time... and with much less effort.

Quick action steps. We create these sites for clients, but you can go to one of the webpage hosting firms, or retain a firm to design and host your site. Either way, follow the guidelines and use it aggressively throughout your search.

"Nothing else in the world... all the armies... is so powerful as an idea whose time has come." —*Victor Hugo*

In our 2009 survey, only 1–2% of 100,000 people indicated they have some version of a personal marketing website, but the percentage is growing rapidly.

At the heart of any professional job search is your need for a step-by-step action plan.

Why do firms like Procter & Gamble and Frito Lay develop marketing plans? It's all about saving time and money instead of selling their products by using hit-or-miss methods.

7 Creating and following a personal action plan

Eliminate trial & error by using a step-by-step action plan.

Over the years, we have seen equally talented people produce widely varying results. One will struggle while the other moves with speed. Those who move rapidly usually have had the benefit of a game plan—a step-by-step track to follow.

In today's competitive arena most people will never get enough interviews with a hit-or-miss approach. This leaves too much to fate. Think of it this way. Chances are you're marketing a "product" with millions of dollars of earnings capacity remaining in your career. That much value deserves your best effort. Besides, job hunting is a numbers game. So, why take a chance at doing a lot of things haphazardly, without a well-designed plan?

Since job hunting is a matter of having the numbers on your side, your action plan should be targeted to produce 25 to 35 responses that result in a phone discussion. The goal is to have several offers maturing at the same time, and you have to be realistic about rejections in the interview process.

Similar to any company who is about to market a new product, a good plan can cut job hunting time in half and save money. It also helps people produce better results, and when people generate a lot of activity in a concentrated time period, they feel better and do better. Much better.

The components of a personal marketing plan

To begin with… (1) Surface the right information about yourself and set clear goals; (2) pinpoint what you should be marketing, especially your transferable skills; (3) identify industry alternatives to target; (4) if you have liabilities, you need strategies to neutralize them; and (5) you need a step-by-step game plan… an action agenda… to get your story told to all the right people. Here's a recap of what our plans cover:

Job hunting goals: Surface all critical information about yourself and then decide on the goals that will advance your career. This includes specific job titles and income goals.

Liabilities & solutions: You need to identify liability issues that might restrict your success… and arrive at ways for minimizing their impact in all written materials and conversations.

Assets, transferable skills & how to market them: All of your assets and skills need to be identified. Then, they need to be incorporated into your resume and letters, and your personal marketing website

Industry alternatives: More and more people are changing industries. The key is to identify industries with characteristics that match those where you have experience.

Action plan for getting interviews: You want to lay out a step-by-step plan… a weekly agenda… that will guide your search. This is your complete track… a game plan. This includes a plan for interviewing and negotiating (your approach to these important matters)… which should be decided on in advance.

What some people say about having a marketing plan

■ *"I felt getting organized, and giving me a clear path to follow, was particularly valuable."*

■ *"My marketing plan was rich with detail. No stone was left unturned. For someone out of work, having a routine and keeping busy is critical."*

■ *"The marketing plan provided a needed structure for my entire job hunting process. It was my reference bible."*

■ *"My marketing plan was similar, but not as detailed as, to what my firm prepares when launching a new product. It seems to be the cornerstone of your philosophy and certainly saved me a great deal of time."*

■ *"I was unemployed for some time and just drifting. Having a marketing plan… a game plan to follow tripled my effort."*

■ *"I don't know what I was thinking of before. Once I had an action plan to follow, it gave a whole new direction to my search."*

■ *"Having a plan reduces the pressure of job hunting."*

Actions you can take to produce interviews

These are all discussed in the sections that follow. However, for the purpose of thinking about your action plan, you might give consideration to the following:

Respond to openings—select as appropriate
■ From 2,000 newspapers
■ From 2,100 trade magazines
■ On 1,500+ job boards
■ On 300,000 employer websites
■ On 3,500 recruiter websites

Contact employers by email, fax or 1st-class mail
Decide if you will follow a "micro" approach, focusing on your best 100 - 200 prospects, and repeatedly working at getting an interview. Or, if your budget allows, use a "macro" approach and make contact with 1,000 firms or more. Some people do both.

■ Decision makers at growth firms
■ Decision makers at other key employers

Contact middlemen by email, fax or 1st-class mail
■ Select from 1,000 premier recruiters
■ Select from 10,000 local and national recruiters
■ Select from 2,800 venture capitalists

Uncover and respond to leads
■ Employers receiving new capital
■ New executive appointments
■ New contracts being awarded
■ Planned relocations announced
■ Record sales and profits achieved
■ Announcements of growth expectations
■ Word of new local business operations

Network on an expanded basis
■ Your contacts
■ Influential alumni
■ Targeted executives by industry

Other
■ Post your resume on job boards
■ Make direct employer contact by phone
■ Pursue "create a job" approaches

No one needs to take all these actions, but a balanced campaign produces better results. The chapters that follow go into more detail on your main options.

Having an action plan can help you get a lot more interviews.

Recapping this chapter. Why do major corporations develop marketing plans to sell their products and services? It's all about saving time and money. Job hunting is a numbers game. And, the more contacts you make... the greater the number of situations that will come your way. Action plans help keep you on track.

Quick action steps. We prepare custom action plans for our clients, but on your own do the following: list your goals, skills, industry options and liability solutions. Then, list all the action steps you're going to use... as reviewed in the following chapters. Relative to contacting employers directly, decide if you will start with a "micro" approach or a "macro" approach.

If you take a micro approach, target your best 100 to 200 prospects, and find a way to keep contacting them until you have a discussion with the right person. Start by sending your material 1st class mail as indicated in chapter 11. Follow up with as many as possible by phone. Then, go back to ones that don't respond with an email letter with a link to your website. Remember, you can also get into these organizations by networking, by using the phone or by following up on a news event about the employer. Continue contacting your best prospects until you can have a conversation with an executive. Follow your plan daily for 8 weeks. Make it your measuring stick.

"It wasn't raining when Noah built the ark." —*Howard Ruff*

"Genius is 1% inspiration and 99% perspiration."
—*Thomas Edison*

It can just be a one-page list with an 8-week schedule, but following a step-by-step plan will make a big difference.

In today's job market you must uncover a lot of openings that are suitable for you.

With attractive ads drawing as many as 300 to 1,000 candidates, besides having a superior resume, you need to uncover a maximum number of openings and respond to them quickly.

8 Finding all the right published openings

You can multiply the openings you uncover by 10 times or more.

It's important to understand how the published job market works. The total market consists of employers who make public their openings... and those who don't. There are five segments to the published market as illustrated in the pie chart below. In the discussion that follows, we will focus on how you can uncover the most number of openings suitable for you... and maximize your activity in this part of the marketplace.

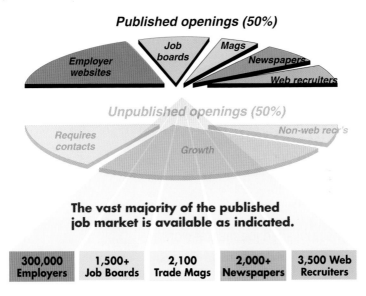

Published openings (50%)

Job boards

Mags

Employer websites

Newspapers

Web recruiters

Unpublished openings (50%)

Requires contacts

Non-web rec'r's

Growth

The vast majority of the published job market is available as indicated.

| 300,000 Employers | 1,500+ Job Boards | 2,100 Trade Mags | 2,000+ Newspapers | 3,500 Web Recruiters |

Understand how many jobs exist at your income level

The Internal Revenue Service tells us that 3% of all Americans report income above $150,000. That means 4.65 million jobs exist at this income and above. But on average, they open up only once every 4 years... because this is how often people change jobs. So, in any given week, there are about 21,000 jobs that become available at this income level.

But these are spread among all 50 states, over 200 industries... and all occupations. So, when executives look for a job at $150,000 or $250,000 or more... what are their chances?

How many jobs are out there in the locations where they live... in their career field... and their industries of interest? Relatively few at any one moment. If you are seeking from $50,000 to $100,000... or $101,000 to $150,000, you will experience a similar challenge. Again, the problem is that the jobs are in all 50 states, 200+ industries and in all professions.

The point you need to understand here is, as a general rule, there are a lot fewer jobs out there than you might think. Uncovering them... and getting considered for them... can be a major challenge. There are contributing factors. The Internet attracts millions to the same popular websites... causing 200 or 300 people to apply for the same opening. And, the "bad" little secret of the Internet is that many of the published jobs... are repeated 10 and 12 times at different websites... and listed long after the jobs are filled. That creates an illusion of far more published openings being out there than the true reality.

How many jobs are out there?... all U.S. jobs by income*

up to $50,000	— 74 %	* Data from the IRS
51,000–75,000	— 11 %	
76,000–100,000	— 6 %	
101,000–200,000	— 7 %	
201,000–250,000	— 1 %	
251,000+	— 1 %	

How the published job market works

When employers decide to hire someone... there is an event that leads to their decision. Typically, someone has retired, quit or been separated. Turnover leads to over 95% of all jobs opening up.

Now once that decision has been made to fill a job, what do employers do first? Well, they look within their company... and they look at candidates on file in their recruiting database. *If they can't fill a job, what do employers do next?* Some consider referrals and those who network their executives. If that doesn't work, they need to go public and see if they can fill their job openings.

This is where the top half of the pie chart on page 69 comes in… "the published job market." This is also where 99% of all job hunters compete. The bottom half is "the unpublished job market," which we will discuss later.

Let's first talk about the published openings and the employer websites. Over 300,000 employers now post their openings. You can also find openings in 2,000 newspapers, 2,100 magazines and over 1,500 job boards.

Newspapers have declined rapidly, but in many instances can still be a good source for lower and mid-level openings for professionals. Employer websites represent the fastest growing means of recruiting staff. There are more than 300,000 employers who recruit this way… and many of them recruit through their website exclusively. The sole exception may be when they go to an executive recruiter for a very senior executive. So, if you've pinpointed your best prospects, check out their websites.

Trade magazines are a worthwhile source for those seeking middle level and upper mid-level openings. Many director and vice president openings, where industry knowledge or experience is important, can still be found in these publications.

In terms of job boards, Monster, Career Builder and Hot Jobs are best known here, but there are many others that might help you. Job boards have replaced newspapers as the largest source for openings. Staffing industry sources now claim that upwards of 40,000 job boards now exist. Our research staff estimates that about 1,500 have some significance. On a broader basis, these can be broken into the following categories:

- Premier job boards
- Manager and executive boards
- Human resources boards
- Finance & accounting boards
- Sales & marketing boards
- Engineering boards
- Diversity boards
- Industry boards
- Military boards
- Scientific boards
- Recent grad boards and state boards

The problem with all the job boards is simple. Once you get past the 200 major boards, most will have only a few listings suitable for you. Even on the largest boards, a person can waste an enormous amount of time, only to find out that there are many duplicate listings, and some appear over and over again for months. By the way, whenever you respond to any type of opening, if you respond by email, also send a response by first-class mail.

Important privacy issues

Once your resume is posted on any number of job boards, you have no idea who may have access to your material. Almost all major job boards sell access to their resume databases. Both employers and recruiters utilize these services as part of their search for candidates. Since every word in your resume is scannable, anyone who uses their services might uncover your resume. This is just one more reason for using short resumes, materials that don't reveal anything unnecessary... on the Internet.

Understanding the aggregators

Aggregators are sites that go out and "spider" other sites... and subsequently list all openings in one place. They by no means represent the entire published market, but these sites make it much more convenient for people to find what they want and respond accordingly.

The major aggregators include: indeed.com, simplyhired.com, advertisedjobmarket.com, and ladders.com. Some sites are free and others charge a fee to subscribe to their service. Currently they claim to aggregate openings from thousands of sources, but none come close to representing the entire published market.

Be aware, the more successful these sites become—the more job seekers compete with you. These sites also must grapple with the problems of all job boards relative to duplicate job listings, false listings and jobs that keep reappearing on a regular basis. In an era of identify theft, you don't want to let complete information fall into the wrong hands. This is another reason for using one-page resumes as your introductory material, and not revealing your complete story.

Over the years some less than legitimate recruiting agencies have been notorious for running ads to simply collect resumes. Then, they try to shop them to employers for a placement commission. Unfortunately, too many people have been burned when their resume reaches their current employer.

Too many online ads are posted which sound like an attractive position, but which subsequently result in a response that asks you to fill out an on-line profile that seeks disclosure of a substantial amount of private information. This is partially caused by the "dehumanization" of the recruiting process in our Internet era. But, be assured, there are others who are collecting this information for different purposes. How do you tell which ads are real? Look for openings that really target what an employer is looking for.

> **"Too many online ads aren't real. They ask you to fill in profiles and disclose a lot of information. The Internet has dehumanized much of the recruiting process."**

Expanding openings you respond to

One way to increase your number of opportunities is to understand the process of upgrading or downgrading ads. For example, a company advertising a Vice President position may be willing to hire an Assistant Vice President or Director, who could move up to Vice President within a year. After all, it isn't so much the title they are after as the skills and talent. That's an example of downgrading the opportunity you see… and encouraging you to respond to situations you might have otherwise bypassed.

By the same token, a firm advertising for a Plant Manager might be persuaded to hire a VP of Manufacturing, provided someone could persuade them such a move would be cost efficient and give added capabilities. That's an upgrade.

Advertised openings can also be used as signals of private openings in other areas of the company. This is called sidegrading.

If, for instance, you see a company hiring a number of sales-people, that's a fairly reliable indicator that they are also hiring people in sales administration, production and other areas.

This approach can be effective for people at lower levels who see openings for senior level positions. Write to the "functional chief" when upgrading, downgrading or sidegrading. HR will typically be the last to know of an emerging job (except in HR).

Compensate for lack of ideal credentials

Don't be restrictive when selecting ads. Employers rarely find the perfect candidate. Try to compensate for any shortfall on credentials through an expression of enthusiasm, or by explaining why you might be well qualified for other reasons. Let the employer know why you selected their ad. *For example:*

... Your company is headquartered near my home.

... I recently read a positive article about your firm... your industry fascinates me.

... My cousin used to be with your company and said it was a great place to work.

... In a similar job I not only got results, but also came in ahead of schedule.

When you find the perfect ad

If you find ads that you think are a perfect fit, use a letter and play back all the items that caused you to feel that way.

Did you ever see an ad and feel "that describes me exactly"? You should follow up on every excellent ad for which you are well qualified. Very few of your competitors will do this.

Keep in mind that using letters alone and following up can help your response rate. Employers who must sift through many resumes start by screening out non-qualifiers. And, since resumes provide more facts, they may work against you. For this reason, when answering ads of special interest, use a strong letter tailored to the requirements of the position.

Sometimes a handwritten note attached to your resume can be effective. This is advisable when there are relatively few points you wish to communicate.

Creative response approaches

One approach is to get additional information, beyond what was in the ad, and use it in your response. This can be achieved by reviewing product literature, websites, annual reports or newspaper articles. Demonstrating industry knowledge works better than anything. Another approach is to develop third-party contacts with employees in the company before responding. Easiest to befriend are sales and marketing managers, public relations staffers or top level executives. Then, you can consider mentioning their names in your correspondence.

Making the most of blind ads

Why do some employers run blind ads? Sometimes blind ads attract employees of competitors. On other occasions they are simply keeping a recruiting assignment private. Some are also meeting advertising contract obligations. Companies also run blind ads to prevent a large number of phone responses or to hide a less-than-attractive reputation. Certain recruiters advertise management positions in blind ads because they need to keep their assignments confidential.

You can't really be sure whether a blind ad represents a real opportunity, but you can't rule out the possibility. So, if you are not worried about the source of the ad, you should respond.

Some ads ask for earnings history. Above $100,000, avoid disclosing history or objectives. Deal with it in your interviews.

Be ready for application forms and tests

■ Avoid completing forms in an office. Never fill them out in a hurry, and always print neatly.

■ When references are requested, delay providing them, but say they will be supplied if mutual interest exists.

■ If a salary objective is requested leave it blank. Stating an objective will only limit your ability to negotiate.

■ When you are asked to list your career history, note brief information and refer people to your resume.

■ Always be sure to reflect an active personality. Mention hobbies, sports, civic and social interests, memberships, etc.

■ Questions along the line of "have you ever been arrested or denied credit," invite a careful response. It is illegal for employers to ask many of these types of questions.

■ When you return your application, always attach a cover letter that clearly restates your interest with enthusiasm.

■ Approach tests with care. Certain tests have fallen into the hands of many people, including your competitors.

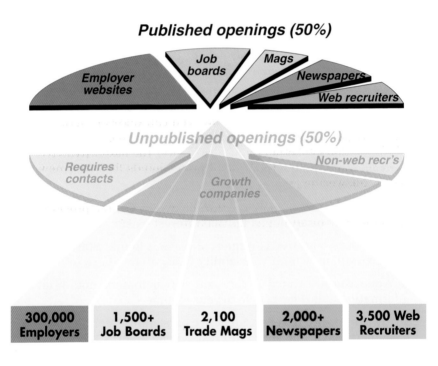

Responding to openings is highly competitive... so you must plan on answering a lot of ads.

Recapping this chapter. Who wouldn't want to uncover as many suitable openings as possible? Now you can uncover virtually the entire published market that's out there for you. But keep in mind that 200–300 others may also answer the most attractive ads, and that only 5% to 7% of all professionals find their new jobs by answering ads.

Quick action steps. Our Job Market Access Center provides access to 97% of all published openings, but if you don't have JMAC, identify the Internet sites you will use regularly, including job boards, aggregators, preferred newspapers, trade magazines and employer sites. Register and upload your resume where appropriate. Set up a system to stay organized.

"Knowledge is power."   *—Sir Francis Bacon*

"A wise man does not trust all his eggs to one basket."
                                             —Cervantes

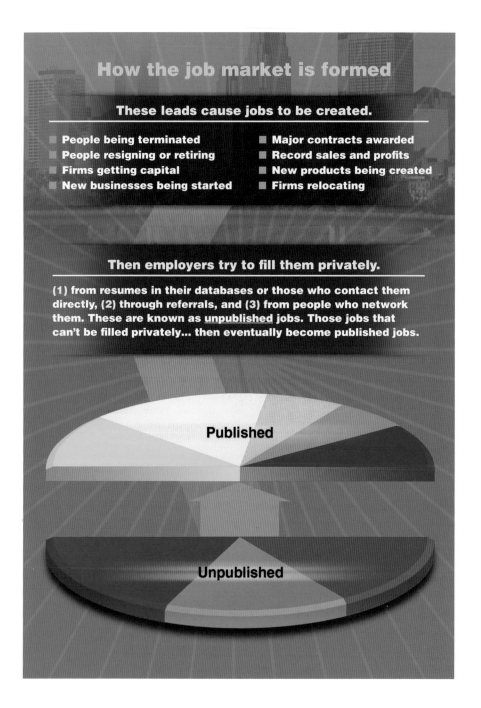

How the job market is formed

These leads cause jobs to be created.

- People being terminated
- People resigning or retiring
- Firms getting capital
- New businesses being started
- Major contracts awarded
- Record sales and profits
- New products being created
- Firms relocating

Then employers try to fill them privately.

(1) from resumes in their databases or those who contact them directly, (2) through referrals, and (3) from people who network them. These are known as <u>unpublished</u> jobs. Those jobs that can't be filled privately... then eventually become published jobs.

Published

Unpublished

9 Make sure you compete for unpublished openings

How to access the right opportunities in the unpublished market.

The bottom half of the chart on the next page is "the unpublished market." One part is the "non-web" recruiters who keep openings private. Here, you need to place a superior resume to generate activity.

Right next to non-web recruiters are the growth companies. This is where the action is in the job market. These firms are constantly hiring. They often offer strong financial packages... and because they are growing so fast, previous industry experience rarely matters. Transferable skills do.

With this in mind, our research staff tracks growth companies... over 10,000 of them, and we often place client resumes with these firms.

Now, for the part of the market that "requires contacts"... if you don't have connections... or cannot network your way in, how do you compete? There are three major ways. One is to get "leads" to these jobs. The other is to place a strong statement of your credentials with "high probability" employers. And the third is to network your contacts, alumni and influential executives.

In addition to requests for interviews, these placements can produce a flow of new telephone discussions that offer networking opportunities. By the way, when you get interviews for jobs in the unpublished segment... how much less competition will you encounter? The answer is... a lot less.

Your best possibilities may be unpublished. These jobs are a mystery to many job seekers. But, there's really nothing mysterious about these openings.

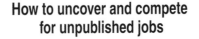

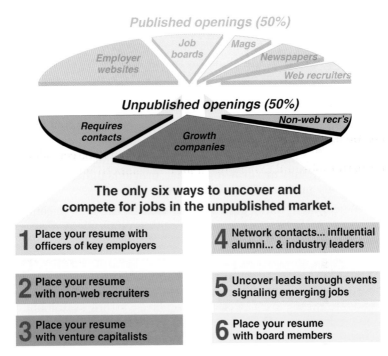

The only six ways to uncover and compete for jobs in the unpublished market.

1 Place your resume with officers of key employers

4 Network contacts... influential alumni... & industry leaders

2 Place your resume with non-web recruiters

5 Uncover leads through events signaling emerging jobs

3 Place your resume with venture capitalists

6 Place your resume with board members

Note: As you can see from the illustration on the page introducing this chapter, events occur that cause jobs to be created. Companies then try to fill them privately, since this is the most economical way searching their databases first. Many, but not all jobs that cannot be filled privately, eventually become published. Keep in mind that the breakdown of the job market changes by income level. The higher you go, the less that are published.

The job market—up to $100K...................... 50% unpublished
The job market—$101K to $150K............... 75% unpublished
The job market—$150K to $200K............... 90% unpublished
The job market—$200K and above............ 95% unpublished

There is much less competition in the unpublished market.

Recapping this chapter. There's nothing hidden about this market. Take advantage of the six ways for uncovering unpublished positions of interest. You can greatly increase the number of interviews you might otherwise get. Plus you will be considered for better jobs and experience a lot less competition.

Quick action steps. JMAC makes this easy for our clients, and one of our divisions can place your materials. You can also do this on your own. First, use directories to identify employers to contact. For up-to-date information on decision makers below CEO level, call employers to ask for that information. Second, place your credentials with the right people in the right organizations.

"Nothing ventured, nothing gained."   *—Anonymous*

"Only those who dare to fail greatly can achieve greatly."
                                        —Robert F. Kennedy

As stated previously in Chapter 9, there are five channels for uncovering published openings. However, you should also focus on getting your credentials into consideration for unpublished jobs. If you really work both the published and unpublished markets, you can get 80–85% exposure for what's out there for you, instead of the 2–3% that most people get.

Connecting with recruiters is still important.

Early in your search place your credentials with all the right recruiters who might have something of interest.

10 Maximizing your recruiter contacts

Market yourself broadly to all the right recruiters.

Whether they are called search firms, contingency recruiters or headhunters, all recruiters work for employers. They screen and recommend prospective employees. These firms *are not* in business to serve job hunters. They fill jobs at $50,000 to $1,000,000 and up. Elite firms are retained at fees averaging up to 33% of compensation.

Executive search firms are referred to as "retained recruiters." Other firms, called contingency recruiters, are active up to $150,000, but operate on commission. Another category is the "temporary or contract recruiter." They earn fees when employers hire professionals on an interim basis.

While 8,000 to 10,000 firms claim to be active, fewer than 50 dominate the upper-end business. Importantly, the best recruiters play a role in helping management set up position specifications.

Regional recruiters have been playing an increasingly important role in the job market. Some specialize by industry... and others by career fields. There are thousands of local recruiters that can be helpful.

Recruiters are typically articulate professionals who have a broad knowledge of business, and are generally excellent marketing executives themselves. It will pay you to develop relationships with those you respect and to maintain them throughout your career. Independent firms that specialize locally or regionally are likely to really know what's going on in their local markets.

Recruiters prefer achievers, people making strong first impressions and who are employed. Being visible in your industry can be key, especially in a hot field or industry. Of course, to develop any level of good activity with recruiters, you'll need superior materials.

When you communicate with recruiters, never be negative about your employer and never appear desperate. Also, keep in mind that recruiters focus on filling their active job listings. So, when you send them a resume, or register online, most of the time if your resume makes the cut, it will simply be scanned into their files.

Direct mail to recruiters

It pays to contact as many recruiters as possible. The vast percentage will not be working on an assignment that might require you... but as time goes by... they may need someone with your background.

When you contact recruiters, be sure to send them a one-page universal resume, suitable for scanning. Cover letters or letter resumes will not play a role. Recruiters will give your resume about 10 or 20 seconds to grab their attention. So you must have a clear objective... and a compelling summary that covers not more than one-third of your one-page resume. But, you don't have to bother with personally addressed letters.

What to expect from resume distributions to recruiters

■ People with recognizable "tickets" do best (for example, well-known schools, degrees, blue chip affiliations, etc.). Distributions will be most effective for those in popular fields (e.g., sales, accounting, finance, IT or IS, manufacturing or service operations and other fields where there is a sizeable demand).

■ Contacting recruiters will be less effective for those in narrow or low demand specialties (e.g., a patent attorney, city manager, technical writer, blood chemist, etc.) or for those making a career change (e.g., an educator moving into business).

■ Also, as you go up the pyramid, there are fewer jobs available, so the response rate will be lower. Those who position themselves with lofty titles, as well as those without recognizable "tickets" who are in narrow demand areas, should expect very little here. It's a low percentage game. Compensating with greater numbers of recruiter contacts is required.

■ Responses come in over weeks and months. A second distribution to the same list three to four months later produces about 80% of the initial response. First class mail does best, followed by fax and email.

■ When responses come in and they engage you on the phone, be ready with a 30- or 60-second commercial highlighting your most marketable features. Keep in mind that you will be most popular with recruiters if you will explore attractive situations, are upbeat and positive about where your career is going, and not openly unhappy about your employer.

Realize that the recruiting business is highly affected by the economy

When times are good, the recruiting industry often soars. This is true relative to the recruiting of professionals at all levels. As a rule the senior executive portion of the market doesn't fluctuate as much as the market from $50,000 to $150,000.

> **"** Less than 8 recruiters or less are contacted by the average professional who seeks a new job. **"**

Because of this, your expectations from placements of your resumes with recruiters should be modest in periods during downturns or recessions.

Occasionally, people mistakenly think that contacting recruiters by phone will be effective. This is rarely the case, in any economy. At all times, you need to keep in mind that recruiters are having conversations with dozens of professionals every day. However, as previously stated, their focus is on filling the limited number of assignments on which they are currently working.

Besides recruiters, venture capitalists can help

A surprising number of VC firms have assumed an active role in hiring for both start-ups and developing firms in which they have an ongoing investment. People who will generate the most interest are normally executives who are candidates for "C" level positions (COO, CTO, etc.) or those who can fill a role as head of a line function (VP Sales, etc.). Others who do well here are primarily in their 30s and 40s. Typically, they've been with major firms and have advanced degrees.

The 40 leading executive search firms*

Battalia Winston
555 Madison Ave Ste 1201
New York, NY 10022-3327
www.battaliawinston.com

Bench International
120 S Doheny Dr
Beverly Hills, CA 90211-2510
www.benchinternational.com

Boyden
50 Broadway
Hawthorne, NY 10532-1245
www.boyden.com

Callan Associates
1211 W 22nd St Ste 821
Oak Brook, IL 60523-3222
www.callanassociates.com

Carlyle Group
625 N Michigan Ave Ste 2100
Chicago, IL 60611-3180
www.carlylesearch.com

Cejka Search
222 S Central Ave Ste 400
Saint Louis, MO 63105-3509
www.cejkasearch.com

Ken Clark International
2000 Lenox Dr Ste 200
Lawrence Township,
NJ 08648-2314
www.kenclark.com

Conley & Company
260 Franklin St Ste 1820
Boston, MA 02110-3164
www.conley.com

Cook Associates
212 W Kinzie St Fl 1
Chicago, IL 60610-4479
www.cookassociates.com

Crist | Kolder Associates
21 W 2nd St Ste 3
Hinsdale, IL 60521-1783
www.cristkolder.com

Cromwell Partners
305 Madison Ave
New York, NY 10165-0006
www.cromwell-partners.com

CTPartners
1166 Ave. of the Americas Fl 3
New York, NY 10036-2738
www.ctnet.com

DHR International
10 S Riverside Plz Ste 2220
Chicago, IL 60606-3707
www.dhrinternational.com

**Diversified Search Ray
& Berndtson**
2005 Market St Ste 3300
Philadelphia, PA 19103-7041
www.diversifiedsearch.com

Howard Fischer Associates
1800 John F Kennedy Blvd
Philadelphia, PA 19103-7421
www.hfischer.com

Furst Group/MPI
555 S Perryville Rd
Rockford, IL 61108-2530
www.furstgroup.com

Gilbert Tweed Associates
415 Madison Ave Fl 20
New York, NY 10017-7939
www.gilberttweed.com

Grant Cooper & Associates
222 S Meramec Ave Ste 202
Saint Louis, MO 63105-3514
www.grantcooper.com

Heidrick & Struggles
233 S Wacker Dr Ste 7000
Chicago, IL 60606-6350
www.heidrick.com

**Hodge / Niederer /
Cariani / Lindsay**
655 Montgomery St Ste 1900
San Francisco, CA 94111-2634
www.hnclsearch.com

*Source: Kennedy Publications

Horton International
29 S Main St Ste 327
West Hartford, CT 06107-2464
www.horton-intl.com

The Howard-Sloan-Koller Group
300 E 42nd St Fl 15
New York, NY 10017-5925
www.hsksearch.com

Isaacson Miller
334 Boylston St Fl 5
Boston, MA 02116-3492
www.imsearch.com

JM & Company
1045 1st Ave Ste 110
King Of Prussia, PA 19406-1358
www.jmsearch.com

Kaye/Bassman
4965 Preston Park Blvd Ste 400
Plano, TX 75093-5141
www.kbic.com

Korn/Ferry
1900 Avenue of the Stars Ste 2600
Los Angeles, CA 90067-4507
www.kornferry.com

Herbert Mines Associates
375 Park Ave Ste 801
New York, NY 10152-0801
www.herbertmines.com

Preng & Associates
2925 Briarpark Dr Ste 1111
Houston, TX 77042-3734
www.preng.com

PrinceGoldsmith
420 Lexington Ave Rm 2048
New York, NY 10170-2003

Rhodes Associates
555 5th Ave Rm 600
New York, NY 10017-9268
www.rhodesassociates.com

Russell Reynolds
200 Park Ave Fl 23
New York, NY 10166-2399
www.russellreynolds.com

Morgan Samuels
9171 Wilshire Blvd Ste 320
Beverly Hills, CA 90210-5516
www.morgansamuels.com

J. Robert Scott
260 Franklin St Ste 620
Boston, MA 02110-3174
www.j-robert-scott.com

Slayton Search Partners
200 W Madison St Ste 2800
Chicago, IL 60606-3498
www.slaytonsearch.com

Spencer Stuart
401 N Michigan Ave Ste 3400
Chicago, IL 60611-4249
www.spencerstuart.com

Stanton Chase
100 E Pratt St Ste 2530
Baltimore, MD 21202-1074
www.stantonchase.com

Strawn Arnold
2508 Ashley Worth Blvd
Ste 150
Austin, TX 78738-5303
www.salainc.com

Tyler & Company
375 Northridge Rd Ste 400
Atlanta, GA 30350-3299
www.tylerandco.com

Witt/Kieffer
2015 Spring Rd Ste 510
Oak Brook, IL 60523-3903
www.wittkieffer.com

Egon Zehnder
350 Park Ave Ste 801
New York, NY 10022-6079
www.zehnder.com

What some people say about recruiters

■ *"I got all I needed from recruiter distributions."*

■ *"My activity with recruiters was for the best quality jobs. Employers who spend the money on recruiting fees value their positions more."*

■ *"Recruiters will work if you have degrees from well-known institutions, and experience with recognizable firms."*

■ *"Recruiters won't produce if you want to change fields."*

■ *"In the past I did very well with recruiters. However, in this economy, companies just are not spending their money in the same way, and listings with recruiters seem to be down."*

What some people say about VCs

■ *"My position came through contacting a venture capitalist in Atlanta. My background is in biochemistry."*

■ *"I would not recommend the VC route for everyone. I am 53 years old, and had very little response because of my age."*

■ *"I had several things emerge with VCs, but all were related to my previous industry experience and my MBA."*

■ *"VCs worked for me. I wanted to make the shift from staff work as a consultant to a line position in general management."*

■ *"Like contacting employers, getting in touch with VCs works only if your materials arrive at the right time."*

■ *"If you contact VCs, the possibilities that come your way will be all from small firms."*

Why not get into the files of a lot of recruiters? It can help you now... and in the future.

Recapping this chapter. Once you have a superior resume, send it by first-class mail and recruiters may scan it into their files. If you are early in your career, you may hear from them for many years. As your career progresses, stay in touch and make yourself easy to find. If you're seeking a middle income position, contact a lot of local recruiters. At the executive level, send your resume to national recruiters. For executives, keep in mind that the chance of one recruiter working on a job that is right for you is very small.

Quick action steps. For our clients, we place their resumes with appropriate recruiters. However, on your own there are several other sources available online. Check for how up-to-date and thorough they are. Spend time on the Internet, download samples where available, and assess this for yourself.

"What we see depends mainly on what we look for."
                                                        —*John Lubbock*

Going direct to carefully targeted employers can be a fast way to get interviews.

Job hunting is all about getting your credentials in front of the right people... at the right times. Lou Holtz once said, *"If you don't make a total commitment to whatever you're doing, then you look to bail out the first time the boat starts leaking."*

11 Making direct contact with employers

Contact all of your high probability prospects on a direct basis.

Why does direct mail work? Every day we all receive direct mail. However bad junk mail looks, the ones you see again and again are working; otherwise, the senders wouldn't be wasting their money.

One thing that makes it work in many cases is that long copy is used. That's what it takes to motivate all of us to action from *unasked-for correspondence.* Here's an example. Let's say a lawn mower shop has a new product. And you and your next door neighbor are both out cutting your lawns on a hot day. However, your lawn mower breaks down.

Then, the mail carrier arrives at both residences with mail that tells you all about a new lawn mower. It gives a long explanation of why it's superior. Now, your neighbor will look at the mailing piece for two seconds and toss it. He isn't in the market for a lawn mower. On the other hand, they have reached you at the right time, you are likely to read it. Now when you job hunt, your situation is similar. You need to reach the right person. No one else counts.

Some people don't believe in direct employer contact. They think that anything you send to an employer is thrown away. Certainly, this has some truth, since the great majority will throw away your materials in seconds.

But if you've ever needed someone with certain skills... then you know you want the easiest way to find a good candidate. And if a good resume or letter reached you at the right time, you would take action on it. Sending the right materials... to the right person... will get the attention of some decision makers. **But, timing is very critical.** You need to reach a decision maker that might be looking for someone like you. Even if your timing is bad, companies scan the resumes of the better candidates into their database. Then, as they develop a need... this is usually the first place they turn. Contacting employers directly allows you to reach potential buyers quickly. If you want... you can reach the entire universe of all your best prospects.

Is there a negative side to using direct mail?

❝ You need to understand the purpose and strategy behind direct contact with employers. It can be a highly targeted way to reach the people who should know about you. ❞

Yes… and that is the cost. But, you need to weigh that… against the cost of failing to uncover appealing opportunities… with which you would never otherwise connect.

Some also worry that direct contact might make you look too desperate and hurt your image. But, this isn't true. If they don't need you, they will throw away your correspondence in seconds… or some may enter it into their database. In other words, it can do some good… but it won't do any harm. One thing is for certain… you will never generate more offers by having fewer people know about you. When more of the right people know about you, more interest will be generated.

Now, you must realize that 99% of the direct marketing you do will always arrive "uninvited" and reach people who never heard of you. That is why you have to have outstanding materials and low percentage expectations… to make it work. **How many people contact companies directly?** Very few. And, most of them won't use superior materials that grab someone's attention… get them interested… and motivate them to make contact.

Direct marketing principles apply to selling yourself

What types of products or services are sold by direct mail? The answer is generally… more expensive products and services. For example, high end real estate… limited edition leather bound book series… collectibles… financial services to high net worth people… major professional fund raising efforts, etc.

These are not mass market items. They are costly items that are rarely purchased… and it takes a lot of copy to explain them… to get a deal closed. The same is true when you as an individual try to sell yourself by direct mail. At the senior level, you may generate initial interest with a letter, but to get the offer closed you will need a full story… generally an executive biography. So, let's look at the principles of selling a person by direct mail.

The first principle is to contact the right person… in the right company. If you disagree, just try sending your resume out to all sorts of the wrong people. Remember, this is about using a laser... not a shotgun. *Now, the question for you is... can you identify all of the right organizations and the right person to contact?* (The process for identifying the people and the companies is what we call "targeting.")

The second principle is that, as already mentioned, it takes a lot of copy <u>to conclude a sale.</u> All you need to do is look at mailings you receive at home... and the amount of words it takes them to convince a small percentage to act. We've learned that the best results are achieved by making initial contact with a curiosity-arousing letter... then having a long story available to close a deal. That's one reason why executive biographies or interview resumes on your personal marketing website need to be available.

The third principle amplifies what we just discussed. Letters usually work better than resumes. ***Why?*** When you write a stand-alone letter, you can be more personal... and avoid disclosure of any liabilities. They must have short paragraphs... 2, 3, or 4 lines... <u>and be personal</u>.

Sending a resume immediately says you are an applicant... so you are right away put in a subordinate position. But sending a letter is a "peer-to-peer" value proposition. *Which do you think someone on the receiving end would respond to the best?*

You also need to use numbers, preferably significant numbers, wherever possible. And, if you're thinking about changing industries or career fields, you might need to have a completely separate resume to eventually make available... because otherwise you won't be able to appeal to the distinctly different audiences that you will be reaching.

The fourth principle is that your writing needs to be very clear. *Everything needs to be done with clarity, short sentences... backed up by impressive facts or arguments... that somehow say that I've done this before for others... and I want to do this for you.* This is not so easy to do... and requires many drafts.

Now the longer your letter or resume is, the more interesting your words and the benefits they convey need to be. So your correspondence really needs to perform two functions. One, it needs to get across the information quickly... two, it needs to keep the person interested so they want to learn more.

If you genuinely have a great story to tell... the initial letter can be as long as you need. However, as you write longer copy, you have to watch out for revealing liabilities or overselling. Your initial correspondence needs to be all positives... opening no doors to potential negatives that may keep someone from responding. When a reader receives your resume or letter, it has to work in the first 20 seconds to keep people reading. Like holding a feather in the wind, it could blow away... or the reader could hold onto it for some time.

About 3,000,000 positions from $50K to $500K+ are filled annually as a result of direct employer contact.

How large should your direct mail campaign be?

You can take either a "micro" or a "macro" approach. A micro campaign should target your best 100 prospects... or at most 200. And if you personally follow up by phone, it can work very well. But, most people seeking $100,000 or more can also benefit by sending 1,000 letters to other secondary possibilities... and if you are an executive, perhaps more. **Why?**

Well, if you went to 200 organizations... how many are likely to need someone like you? Let's assume that you're looking for a job of which there is **only one** in each organization. For example, let's say you want to be a General Counsel... VP of Sales... Director of HR... the CFO... VP of Operations... the CEO, etc. On the average, one company out of each 208 is likely to need someone like you at that moment. However, they may be in the wrong industry for you. And, even with the best materials, they may not be as impressed with your background as you think they should be.

Here is why the previous paragraph is so true. The job market runs primarily on turnover. From the *U.S. Labor Department*, we know that professionals and executives change jobs at the rate of once every four years in the U.S. That means that the job they occupy becomes available once every four years... or 208 weeks. So, that's why we know that if you went out to 208 companies, you would probably only reach one that needs someone like you right now.

If you went out to 1,000, you would reach five. And, if you went out to 3,000, you would reach 15. And if you went out to 10,000, you would probably reach 50. But, because they would be in many industries... and because they would reflect many different personal preferences—they wouldn't all react well to your particular background or presentation.

Does anyone ever go out to 3,000... 5,000 or 10,000? The answer is yes... and quite often. Who are they? They are usually senior level people who can move across many industries... like executives in HR... sales... accounting... CFOs... general managers... or simply those who are specialists at building or turning around companies... or who can bring leadership ability to almost any firm.

Can you contact more than one executive in a firm?

The answer is yes—particularly when contacting larger companies. Let's look at three examples:

Example #1. Years ago, our firm had an executive come to us who had been a sales manager in the camera industry. He contacted us with only one objective in mind. He wanted to be the national sales manager for a specific Japanese firm.. So, we wrote an initial letter... a short resume as a one-page summary (a universal resume) and a full biography for him... and we had them translated into Japanese. It presented a very compelling statement as to why he was the ideal candidate to run American sales operations. Initially, we sent that document to the head of Pentax operations in Japan. That didn't work. Subsequently, we sent it to several other executives, including the CFO, the EVP and the CEO. Eventually the top executive flew him over to Japan and some weeks later he got the job.

> **If you know of a large employer that would be a good fit for you, be sure to develop a strategy to contact a variety of people who might get you in the door for an interview.**

Example #2. Another executive we once handled wanted to live in Rochester, New York and had a specific interest in the Xerox Corporation. Over a period of ten weeks, we contacted more than 15 different executives... before an interview was secured. Surprisingly, it never came to light that we had contacted other executives in the same corporation. The same would be true of most large organizations today.

Example #3. In another instance, a client in New Jersey, who had both marketing and technical skills, sent his materials to the HR Department plus five other decision makers in different divisions of a large pharmaceutical company. The HR Department responded that they had distributed his resume throughout the firm and there were no suitable openings. Over the next 10 days, he learned in follow-up calls that two other recipients were not interested, but one was and invited him for an interview. He also received two replies in writing. One said they might have an opening in the next two months. The other invited him for an interview right away... because he seemed to be a good match for a position they wanted to fill soon. Without direct mail, none of this would have happened.

Can you go back to the same executive?

The answer is yes. Let's take an example of a CFO who lost his job, but wanted to continue living in a medium size metro area like Denver. Now, let's also assume the executive wants to earn $200,000. So, we might start by looking at the size of companies in Denver... according to their number of employees... who might require a CFO and who would also be able to pay him or her $200,000 or more. Listed below are the approximate number of employers in the Denver area... with a population of approximately 2.7 million.

Less than 10 employees =	85,000
11-20 employees =	10,000
21-50 employees =	6,000
51-100 employees =	3,000
Greater than 100 employees =	2,500

Chances are that we would need to restrict ourselves to organizations with more than 100 employees... or 2,500 organizations. So let's now apply the math that we discussed earlier. Based on turnover data, how many companies might have the job we're looking for become available this week? If you divide 2,500 by 208, you'll get about 12 companies. However, keep in mind that we are referring to jobs becoming available (or needs evolving into jobs) this week. If our executive client is in the market for 12 weeks, there would be a total of 12 x 12... or about 144 positions available during this time period. That's why it pays to have your material good enough so it gets scanned in their databases.

We have learned that if we go back to the same organizations and executives... a second time within 90 days... that the response we get will range as high as 75% of whatever activity we got the first time.

Can direct mail create a job and be worth the expense?

The answer is yes to both questions. It is important to remember the higher you go, the more likely your desired position will be found somewhere in the unpublished market. And, the greater the chance that a job will be created or reshaped to fit your particular blend of skills and strengths... and the specific contributions you can make.

Here's an example. A COO with achievements in both sales and marketing, attracted interest in the aviation, defense and electronic industries. At the end of his search, he had ten attractive opportunities to negotiate. One of those was with a company that he highly respected, but the original position they had in mind was not big enough for him. Importantly, he did not allow the conversations to end there, because he liked the company.

So, he went the extra mile to go through three meetings. At the conclusion, the job had been redefined to two levels higher... in order to take advantage of his many strengths. It also carried a base salary $100,000 larger than the original job.

There is much more to marketing any professional or executive on a direct basis than can be covered in this brief discussion. It remains, however, one of the quicker ways for any person to uncover unpublished positions... that would have otherwise never been uncovered. In addition, you gain the long-term advantage of getting into the databases of organizations... and paving the way for an inquiry sometime in the future. This can be very important for young professionals who will have a number of career moves ahead of them.

Why go direct to employers... if you can get response ads?

That is for you to decide. Interestingly, in the example above, several of the executive's 10 opportunities were from ads and recruiters... while the balance were from direct contact with board members and employers. But, if you elect not to go direct to employers, you can only speculate as to what you left out there undiscovered.

What's the least expensive way?

Your choices are making contact by **(1)** email... **(2)** fax... or **(3)** first-class direct mail. Going to someone's personal email is inexpensive, but sometimes offends people. Sending them a note through a corporate email address works best in smaller firms. Making contact by fax can be effective and relatively inexpensive... if you can get access to a fax that goes to them. *(The problem in large firms is that your fax may never reach the right person.)* Using the general fax number in a small or medium sized company works better. Contacting executives by first-class mail in an envelope marked "private and personal" is the best way but is also the most expensive. As a rule, to have a mailing service do this will cost $2.00 or more per letter.

Granted, that means $2,000 to make 1,000 contacts. But what is the value of uncovering those handful of senior executive openings... and having them be interested in you? Another way to look at it is to consider how much money you may be losing by staying unemployed for just an extra month. So, for many people, the value is high. And, of course, these job hunting expenses are generally tax deductible.

I asked a friend of mine, a CEO of a high tech company, what he thought of direct mail. His response was, *"Well, I get a lot of resumes and even some from my board members who pass on candidates. It works if the person really comes across well."* Another friend, a VP of Marketing at a Fortune 500 company, put it another way. He said, *"I look at resumes. If something matches my needs, I usually respond directly. It's a matter of timing."*

A third associate, the head of HR at a Fortune 500 company, sent me the following when I was updating this book. His comment was, *"I would highly recommend direct mail. Third-party letters can be especially effective if the right person is writing for you. Just prepare a letter they approve for their signature. Make it easy for them to assist."*

Direct mail actions that work best

Let's assume you were a district sales manager seeking a national sales manager's job. Here is a range of direct mail actions you might consider taking.

■ **Most popular.** Sent to CEOs. Takes good credentials in mainstream fields to work. Response is from large firms, but better from small companies.

■ **Much better.** Sent to SVP sales by personal name, selected by industry, size and location. Can be very good with telephone follow-up.

■ **Excellent.** Sent to SVP sales to whom you have spoken. Or, sent to SVP sales, by name, where a third-party mailing goes out under someone's letterhead.

■ **Outstanding.** Sent to SVP sales, by name, to whom you've been referred or met or spoken to.

■ **Often the best.** Doing continuous direct mail to your high probability prospects. For example, if no interest results from a first mailing, contact a minimum of five other decision makers in mid-sized firms and up to 12 in large organizations or divisions—spaced out over eight weeks (*with phone follow-up*).

> ❝ If you can afford it, large scale but well-targeted personal letters, sent by first-class mail and marked private and personal... can be the single fastest way to get a new job. But, there are no guarantees. ❞

Selecting your targeted list

Let's review principles that have made direct mail successful. First of all, you must reach the right person. So, you need to compile a list of your highest probability targets by industry and location. For senior executives, we suggest focusing on the CEO or board members of firms in target industries. Now, in a very large firm, you may be unsure whom to contact. People with varying titles, for example... Group VP, North American Operations, may be running several divisions or business units.

If possible, research the specific decision maker who would be most interested in your message. As an alternative, it can sometimes be appropriate to contact the CFO. He or she may be aware of opportunities across operations... and may have the ear of the CEO.

Direct mail response is best for small and mid-sized firms. In large organizations, you will want to consider multiple mailings to different executives. In one case, approaching an employer with 28,000 employees in one metro area, each week, for 12 weeks, we mailed to a decision maker in the firm—until an interview was secured.

In smaller firms, target owners or top officers. They can be decisive and make hiring decisions more quickly. Follow-up mailings after 90 days will generally produce 75 to 80% of the response of your original mailing.

Contacting board members is worth separate comment. When you do this, it has to be done in a dignified manner with the correct style and tone. Our approach is to send out custom letters under our letterhead each week. For each executive, we include a custom cover letter with a universal resume for a short overview and an executive biography for a more extensive recitation. This lets board members have a thumbnail sketch and an extensive recitation of your credentials and abilities in your executive biography. This presentation is similar to a board briefing book that a member would receive prior to a board meeting.

10% of your "macro" list should be your "best-of-best" possibilities, worthy of follow-up and repeat mailings. 20% should be "primary" possibilities and the balance "secondary."

What some people say about direct employer contact

■ *"Targeted third-party mailings were critical. They went out under the names of close friends, and the response was excellent."*

■ *"Mailings went out to 1,000 companies. Response was low, but after six weeks yielded two good offers."*

■ *"My recommendation for your clients in a narrow industry segment is direct mail first, and networking second."*

■ *"We did several thousand mailings in foods and pharmaceuticals. Results have continued for months. "*

■ *"I live in Columbus, Ohio and could not move. I used custom mailings, emerging opportunities and networking."*

■ *"Mailings were more important for me because I did not want to rely on my contacts. A total of 6,000 mailings went out under the names of three close friends."*

■ *"I've been an HR executive many years. Very few people who look for a job realize that contacting employers directly should be part of almost every search."*

■ *"You have to accept that your response here will be very low, and then you have to make the most of every opportunity. The situations that come your way here are superior and less competitive, and the employers can reach decisions faster."*

A successful letter to an employer

Dear Mr. Pepper:

P & G's leading position in the food industry has been of great interest to me for some time. This, along with your well known reputation for attracting the best marketing talent, has prompted this letter.

In my current role of Marketing Manager for General Foods, I launched a new breakfast product. I am sure it is familiar to you, and it succeeded despite fierce competition. Under my direction, it captured 13% of the market. The brand is now well poised for additional growth.

Having accumulated nine years of similar successes, I now feel ready to assume broader responsibilities as a Vice President of Marketing.

While I am happy with General Foods, such growth opportunities will not be possible because of organizational reasons. However, recent articles have left me with the sense that my timing may tie in well with your plans.

Of additional importance, I have always had an interest in living in Cincinnati. In fact, last month I spent a wonderful week competing in the Lake Caldor classic. This, along with some close friends, convinced me that we would like to relocate to your beautiful city in the near future. You can review my background in more detail on my website at www. mitch@yahoo.com.

On Monday I will call your secretary to see if a convenient meeting can be arranged.

Very truly yours,

Mitch Watson

Mitch Watson

A successful letter to an employer

Dear Mr. Jones:

Can I help you build your sales? I've helped others as both a consultant... and as a full-time executive.

My skills are in sales management... recruiting sales organizations... personal sales production... and key account management. I can build sales organizations from the ground up... or take them to the next level.

My titles have included managing partner... executive vice president... and president of my own firm—but I value contributing, building sales and building profits.

Others have commented on my strong verbal and written skills, my personable nature and my capability for working closely with top executives. All my life I've been hands on, but I'm very capable of handling small and large staffs... and budgets.

My industry experience covers real estate, HR organizations, commercial finance and non-profit organizations. The industry has never made much difference—it's the skills and fresh thinking I bring to the table.

With a BS in Business Administration, I've also been a strong personal sales producer. In closing, if you're looking to build your sales volume, I would enjoy speaking with you at your convenience. You can reach me at (201) 445-9182 or you can email me at henry@yahoo.com.

Very truly yours,

Henry Larimer
Henry Larimer

A successful letter to an employer

Dear Mr. Perkins:

I was quite struck by the article about your new sales philosophy. My qualifications would seem to be a perfect fit for your type of organization.

As a District Sales manager, I set up a branch office for a company in the office products industry. Under my leadership, sales increased 23% and 58% respectively in the first two years of operation.

I believe I could do as well for you... and I'd like to try. My immediate interest is in obtaining a Regional Sales Manager's position that offers superior potential for a young person who can prove her value to Microsoft.

My background also includes administrative and supervisory responsibilities in the areas of hiring, training and motivating people.

I'm single, 29 years old and have a B.A. degree from Indiana University. There I was elected Student Body President and graduated third in my class.

May I have the opportunity to further discuss my qualifications during a personal interview? A more detailed summary of my background can be viewed at my website, www. lreilly.com. I would look forward to speaking with you and will call your secretary on Wednesday to see if a convenient meeting can be arranged.

Sincerely,

Lynne Reilly

Lynne Reilly

A successful letter to an employer

Dear Mr. Walters:

For a number of years I have been associated with a firm that is somewhat related to your industry. In line with this, I thought you might be able to direct me to an appropriate executive in your firm who I could help.

I am an experienced corporation lawyer. My career has spanned a broad range of legal functions involving substantial responsibility and sensitivity.

Most recently, I assisted in a major acquisition, and in the restructuring of a company under Chapter XI. In the course of my work, I uncovered millions of dollars in credits that had been unrecognized.

Prior to this, I developed the Budweiser franchise agreement. It is the standard against which all agreements are measured. I have a BA from Hobart and a Law degree from NYU. I am a member of the New York Bar.

I have much more than a passing familiarity with your business. Furthermore, I want to find a new position where I can make the best use of my expertise. I am willing to travel or relocate as the situation might require.

I would appreciate an opportunity to bring my qualifications to the attention of your senior executives who might benefit from my experience. I will call you next Monday to see if you can suggest the right people for me to contact.

Sincerely,

Thomas Singleton

Thomas Singleton

A successful letter to venture capitalists

Dear Mr. Miller:

I know from past discussions with venture capital firms that you often need to search for second-stage management. My second stage growth and turnaround achievements are significant.

By way of introduction, as a Fortune 500 executive and marketing leader, I have enjoyed a classical marketing and management career including key positions with well known firms and brands.

These include Lever Brothers, Lipton, Borden and Good Humor. My experience encompasses growth through such positions as Director of Product Management, Marketing Director, Senior Vice President of Sales and President.

Entrepreneurial by nature, I have more than a decade of experience in start-ups and turnaround management. I have consistently increased sales, expanded market share, reduced costs, and streamlined operations.

As a venture capitalist, your ear is close to the ground regarding new business opportunities in the consumer product area. With that in mind, I am requesting a brief meeting in which we could exchange industry knowledge.

I will contact you in a few days to determine a time when we can meet. Thank you in advance. A detailed biography is attached.

I look forward to speaking with you soon.

Sincerely,

Larry Morgan

Larry Morgan

■ Contacting employers is what job hunting is all about. Yet, it is surprising how few professionals and executives bother contacting firms they would enjoy working with on a direct basis.

■ First, you should get the names of the decision maker you should contact. Then, decide whether to make contact by email, fax, direct first class mail or by phone.

Direct marketing yourself is like selling a high end service. It can work... but it takes numbers.

Recapping this chapter. When you contact employers directly, you must reach the right person who might be in the market for someone like you. No one else counts. Large scale efforts as well as small custom mailings can work. The right targets, materials and timing are all important. The higher your income, the more connections you need to make and the lower your percentage response is going to be. Best response comes from custom first-class mail. Fax distributions are second... followed by email.

Quick action steps. Our clients can take advantage of the many databases available through JMAC. On your own, you can use other sources. Use the guidelines to contact the right decision makers with employers who are high probability prospects for you. Follow up on the phone with your very best targets. Contact board members and venture capitalists, if appropriate.

"Life is an echo. What you send out—you get back."
—George Santayana

"Progress always involves risk. You can't steal second base and keep your foot on first."   *—Frederick B. Wilcox*

"You'll always miss 100% of the shots... you don't take."
—Wayne Gretzky

When you uncover leads, you can get in the door first.

It only stands to reason that the earlier you can find out about a job possibility, the greater the advantage you will have.

12 Making sure you uncover leads

You can uncover leads to emerging jobs before they are released.

Every day, events occur in tens of thousands of firms that lead decision makers to begin the process of privately looking for new people. These events are often reported in local and national publications, newsletters and online. They are essentially signals of emerging jobs... and that hiring will soon follow. What kinds of news events signal emerging jobs?

- An employer receiving new capital
- A firm kicking off a new product
- Executive appointments
- Word of new local business operations
- New contracts being awarded
- Planned relocations
- Major licensing agreements
- Announcements of growth expectations
- Announcements of record sales & profits

For companies undergoing transitions, chances are they will need to attract good people to handle problems or capitalize on their opportunities. Their activities won't just be limited to one or two functions. They can be expected to need people in all categories: sales, marketing, finance, etc. What's more, these situations will generally be much less competitive than published openings.

Ripple effect thinking

When you read about a company that is giving out signals that they may be hiring at an above-average rate, don't stop at the obvious implications. Use what we refer to as "ripple effect thinking." This is simply taking the time to think about changes that may be occurring in the company up and down the line and across many functions.

You may also get some good ideas about using information to find opportunities with a company's suppliers, customers and even their competitors. Consider the following example.

An obvious "emerging" opportunity

You read that a firm is starting a new division to sell a revolutionary cell phone… one that can compete with the iPhone and the Blackberry. The obvious implications are that this company could very well need people in marketing and sales. Since it's a new division, you might also expect that there will be some need for finance people as well.

If you're a design engineer, you might also project a need for that capability to support the design effort. Those possibilities would be real enough, but now let's use "ripple effect thinking" to see if we can infer some other needs. If you're an industrial engineer with knowledge in this product area, you know this concept will concern competitors. You might contact them to help in the new product area.

Or, you may be someone who is experienced in dealing with regulatory authorities. You recognize that the potential customers for this product will have to deal with the FCC to gain product approval. Consequently, this firm might need someone like you.

Don't ignore firms with problems

Reorganizations involve shifts in executive ranks. They spell opportunity for those at the next lower level, and changes ripple through the organization down the line. Problems often imply one of two things: managers haven't been performing well, or the company needs new capabilities to survive and grow. Organizations with problems often need help from the following:

- Marketing people who can identify new markets and find new applications for existing products.

- Sales people who can help increase revenues.

- Applications engineers who can design new products… and applications for existing ones.

- Operations and manufacturing people who can find more cost-efficient ways to produce goods and reduce overhead.

- Skilled negotiators who can win more favorable terms with labor, suppliers and customers.

- Financial staff who can cut costs or raise more capital to make further expansion possible.

- Real estate and financial people who can redeploy assets or dispose of unwanted facilities.
- CEOs, COOs and GMs who can take responsibility for plant closings, consolidations and streamlinings.
- CEOs and COOs who can supply new leadership.
- HR executives who can help find all these people.

How some people got jobs through leads

"I saw that a group of CPAs had formed a new firm here in Kansas City, which was near my home. Less than three weeks after contacting them, I started my new job in accounting."

"I read that a troubled manufacturer was divesting a division to raise cash. I called the new president. I am now CFO."

"My previous job was as a GM. I read that an investment was being made in our area. I got through after three attempts to the CEO."

"I wanted to work in the sports marketing field and saw a lead about a partnership investment of a top basketball player."

"I had felt that age would be a big problem. With a good story and materials, I had all the interviews I needed from leads."

"As a former CFO I knew I could help companies in trouble. So, getting good leads was relatively easy and was my primary focus."

"I wanted a chance in sales. When a nearby firm was acquired, I sent a letter to the top sales executive at the acquiring firm."

"I saw that an auto firm was investing in our area of Alabama. I got an interview with the General Counsel."

"I was an administrator of a university hospital. One of your leads was about a hospital supplier and I soon started in a new job."

"For me, as a manager with more than 20 years experience, working leads had the highest payoff, and it is far less competitive."

A successful letter to a lead... an emerging opportunity

Dear Mr. Cavanaugh:

Today's New York Times indicated you are looking to acquire firms that are sound in concept, but are losing money in the current economy.

Although not a "miracle worker," I have 20 years of solid experience in growing small companies and larger industry leaders. I have consistently applied sound strategies to turn around profitability and revitalize sales.

Most recently, in my position as Vice President of Marketing for KLX Software in Seattle, I rebuilt a direct sales force, expanded distribution channels, and developed and launched new products. As a result, I improved market share by 20%, and increased sales by $40 million in the first year.

In a previous position at Decision Dynamics, Inc., I revamped a poorly designed marketing plan to increase sales. In the first year I achieved $2.5 million in new orders alone.

My success in achieving bottom line results stems from putting in place assertive, yet practical, action plans.

Confident that I have the experience and personal dynamics to move struggling companies to growth and profitability, I would appreciate the opportunity to meet with you to discuss how my background could meet the needs of companies in which you have an important financial stake.

I look forward to speaking with you soon. My biography is attached.

Sincerely,

Marty Paulson

Martin Paulson

For writing brief memos or emails, linking to your personal marketing website, or attached to your resume—in response to a news event

Congratulations on your appointment as VP of Sales. A brief review of the attached resume will indicate a few reasons why I think I can be of help.

The article in the Dallas News was fascinating. I thrive on challenges involving cost control. Also, as the attached resume illustrates, I handled several turnarounds.

Today's news indicated that you're expanding in Georgia. Maybe I can help. As you can see from the attached resume, I've had five years of solid experience in plant operations.

If getting results is the main qualification for the job you described in The New York Times, the attached resume will indicate that I have consistently demonstrated that ability.

I would like to have the opportunity to tell you how my energy, plus years of experience in your field, can be a winning combination for you.

I have been inspired by the leadership repeatedly demonstrated by your company, and would like to put my own interest and knowledge to use for the firm. May I hear from you?

The challenges you described are ideally matched to the skills I have developed. On top of that, I can bring you the benefits of years of experience and accomplishment in the industry.

My background is a perfect match for the qualities you are looking for to manage the new division. My resume will support this, and I am very much interested in your company.

Your company was recommended to me by a friend who saw today's article in the Chicago Tribune. May we have a brief talk?

Congratulations on the design breakthrough of the P400. That is the reason for my brief note.

Congratulations on your promotion to President. Perhaps you could use a strong _____ financial assistant.

When you're looking for a job, acting on leads should be one of your key strategies.

Recapping this chapter. Using "leads" to find emerging jobs is not widely understood… but it is a highly effective way to find and compete for unpublished jobs.

Quick action steps. Through JMAC we stream daily leads via email to our clients. On your own be sure to read relevant business journals. You can also research sites where you can access news from employers by state and industry. Select the business news most helpful and follow our principles.

"Every man is the architect of his own fortune."   *—Sallust*

"In the long run, we shape our lives. And the choices we make are ultimately our own responsibility."   *—Eleanor Roosevelt*

Only 1% of all job seekers go after emerging jobs. When you act on a lead from an "event," you will encounter far less competition. You may even be first in the door.

Networking is getting a lot easier.

Now you can network even when you have a limited base of connections...
and you can do it fast.

13 Networking in a much easier way

Now you can network by using an entirely new and faster approach.

Networking is a pyramiding strategy... one where you capitalize on one name to gain an interview with another. The most popular style of networking involves seeking *informational interviews.*

Your purpose here would be to get an appointment with executives and ask them to share with you some information about their industry challenges. Naturally, if you happened to be well connected, and you maintained a list of contacts into the hundreds, that could help give you a fast start.

Unfortunately, the problem with this is that it usually takes a long time. And, some people find it demeaning to approach friends and acquaintances to ask for help in finding a new career position. Nevertheless, it does work if you have the time and inclination to approach your job search this way. Hopefully, some of your discussions will result in referrals to another executive who might have something for you... and be able to use your talents.

While this traditional networking can work, besides taking time, networking people with a new job in mind has become overworked. Just about every executive has been networked over and over again. What's more, who has 45 minutes to an hour to devote to someone else? Or even 30 minutes?

Networking the new way

The growth of the Internet and social networking sites such as LinkedIn, Zoominfo, Zing and others, combined with personal marketing websites and the use of email... are ushering in a new era of networking. And, it is a much easier and more effective way to network.

All you need are some superior resumes and an attractive personal marketing website that display your formal credentials, accomplishments and transferable skills in an impressive way. Then, instead of asking for "an informational interview," you can just send off a well designed email with a link to your website.

People on the receiving end will get it and be impressed and you will have their time. And, you can use this method to contact hundreds of people in a very short time... people who have a high probability of being able to help you.

What kind of people? I'm not suggesting that you do this with your genuine personal contacts and real friends, who will look forward to visiting with you on a personal basis. However, they would also be very interested in seeing your personal marketing website.

> **❝**Only 6% of all professionals network more than 15 people. Now you can do that in less than an hour.**❞**

But we all have what I refer to as acquaintances on another level. Here I'm referring to people who might be golfing partners, politicians, lawyers, ministers, investment bankers, etc., people who might legitimately be able to easily refer us to others based on a short telephone call *(after seeing your personal marketing website)*.

You can also target industries of interest and get contact information on key executives who would be good targets. Influential alumni have also proven to be very responsive to this approach.

Other possibilities to contact include executive directors of associations who have many "lines" into their industries. Editors of business magazines and newsletters may also have an inside track on the needs of specific organizations.

Other good executives to target can be those who have been quoted in articles. This makes an introduction easy and natural. Also be sure to track down lost contacts in past organizations.

As far as informational interviews go, you can do that while abiding by some time tested rules. For example, your discussions must be kept brief, and you need to have your list of questions prepared. You will do better when you have researched a firm and are asking for feedback on ideas that may benefit them.

Networking through references

Mark was a VP who wanted to become a CFO. We helped make Mark aware of the power of his references. When Mark heard his company was to be sold, he felt his salary was $20,000 less than it should be.

Did his boss feel bad about paying him less than he was worth? Absolutely. Could Mark ask him to act as a reference, and would he raise him to the level he wanted, in return for staying for the last two months? Definitely.

Now, the boss had a friend in an accounting firm. Mark asked his boss if he would approach his friend as a second reference. Together, they had lunch. The accountant was happy to be a second reference. In the same way, Mark developed a third reference, his own brother-in-law.

When he launched a campaign, he had a good interview with the president of a small paper company. A conservative man, he asked for three references. Mark recontacted his references, so they were ready. After his boss had given him a glowing reference, the president mentioned that he was still uncertain.

When the second reference was called (the boss's friend), he told the president that in the right situation Mark could help save $1 million in taxes, and control costs. He had repositioned Mark as a broader-based financial executive.

Next, Mark's third reference supported the others and added a few points. The day after the last reference check, he got a call from the president, and guess what? His message was, *"Mark, what will it take to get you?"* He ended up as CFO at a much higher income.

Selecting your references

Most of the time, important references will be the people you reported to in the past, or the person you currently report to or their superiors. Choose the highest level reference, as long as you get an enthusiastic endorsement, and avoid people who don't communicate well. Also be sure to give them an idea of what to emphasize about your background.

References you select should know your achievements and have no hesitation in making strong statements. What they say is very important, but the enthusiasm and conviction they project is more important. Let them know that you have high regard for them and their opinions, and they will want to do their very best.

Also, make sure that your references know the full story. Here's an example. A woman who worked for me left to complete her MBA. She was competent, had a quiet manner, but could be forceful. When she started interviewing, she brought me up-to-date. She called after an interview to tell me that she felt they had some concerns about her quiet nature.

Armed with that information, I was ready when I was called by her potential boss. Before the question was asked, I mentioned that sometimes people could be deceived by this woman's quiet nature, but that she could be very assertive. The person responded that I had put to rest his one concern.

References can be your best sources of referrals. Leave each person a half-dozen resumes. Reassure them that you won't use them too many times. After calling them, send a brief note that shows your appreciation and summarize a few positive things they can say about you. You can even make a list of questions that employers might ask and suggest answers for them.

By the way, let references know as soon as you have used their names, and ask them to let you know when they have been contacted. Employers will sometimes ask them for the name of someone else who is familiar with you.

Handling questionable references

If someone is likely to give you a bad or lukewarm reference, you need to bring it out in the interview and supply enough good ones to offset it. For example, if the interviewer asks to speak with a reference who will be questionable, defuse the situation by explaining that you had differences of opinion on company directions. Remain totally objective and unemotional, and never imply negatives about that person. Also, if you are doubtful about what a reference might say, you might have a friend do a mock reference check to find out what is being said.

If the reference is neutral, don't hesitate to ask the person to furnish more positive information. If necessary, explain that any negative input is keeping you from winning a position and enabling you to support yourself and your family. As a last resort, you may have to imply that you will seek a legal remedy.

Fundamental guidelines for executive networking

■ Only network with superior materials. List people you want to see, in industries of interest, and find a way to meet them.

■ Always know what you want to say, the questions to ask, and the strengths to emphasize.

■ Be sure to exchange cards and talk with people wherever you go. Let them know you are thinking about something new.

■ Try to leave every meeting or discussion you have with new names.

■ Always remember the names of the front office and send a non-standard thank you note after each meeting. For example, mention an article you have seen where the firm is mentioned.

■ Remember, people know when they're "being networked." That doesn't mean they won't help, but don't try to fool them.

What some people say about our networking approach

■ *"I have never been comfortable networking and for this reason have always been reluctant to contact associates about looking for a job. However, having a personal marketing website and sending emails made me a convert, and it works."*

■ *"Networking was essential for me. Before using your system, I never felt comfortable with the process, since I didn't like asking for help. This time I sent out the CEO biography with a cover letter to 150 people. More than 10 percent gave me leads."*

■ *"I wanted to be in the high-end furniture business, and my wife has a decorating business. Using your materials, we worked on her connections and my own, using two personal marketing websites. I had my first offer in six weeks, and a second 10 days later, and I have joined Drexel in a top sales position."*

■ *"What I discovered was that having a great website where my material could be viewed made networking an entirely different effort. When they saw my site, I found people helpful and interested. Most important, I developed a lot of situations to look into with your approach."*

■ *"My goal was to join an airline in a finance position. Having been an Air Force pilot gave me an advantage, but the key was networking, getting out emails that linked to my website, and using the phone. The position I accepted was with an airline."*

■ *"Your system did a lot for me, but what really helped the most was learning how to use my 1500 person Rolodex here in New York. My materials were excellent, but the personal marketing website gave me an instant distribution system, and it multiplied my contacts many times over. I got a job as executive director of a large nonprofit. I had activity from many sources, but the best were through networking."*

A sample networking letter to an old friend

Dear Sherrill,

It isn't often, unfortunately, that I write letters to old friends. There's a good reason for doing so now and it involves a favor.

As you may know, I have had a successful consulting practice over recent years. However, I have decided to seek out a new line assignment as president of a small corporation, or as marketing executive with a larger firm.

As part of this new direction, I am interested in expanding my acquaintances at the level of CEO. Considering your long history in the area, it seems that you may be able to provide me with a few select introductions.

Ideal contacts would be with CEOs of firms having significant growth potential. A company facing a turnaround situation could also be interesting.

In any event, I hope to move swiftly in securing appropriate contacts. With this in mind, I am including a link below to my personal website listing my credentials. Please feel free to forward it to others.

Please give my best regards to Phil. Thanks in advance for your time.

With my best regards,

Gordon Edwards

Gordon Edwards

A sample letter for requesting a reference

Dear Dr. Sovern:

It seems like years since we last talked, but I hope that all is well with you. Since graduating from Columbia my career has taken some interesting turns.

For the first three years I worked as an assistant to the PR director at Merrill Lynch. My earnings there allowed me to finance a graduate degree.

Two years ago a unique opportunity was made available to me from the Clairol Corporation. Despite my relatively young age, I now have two years experience as manager of PR.

Unfortunately, it looks as though the company will be sold in the next few months. As part of our impending merger, all staff positions will be under review, and that prompts this letter.

If it is convenient, I would like to use you as a reference in case I do need to consider a new move. To bring you up to date I am including a link to my personal marketing website… so that you can review my most recent resume. Any thoughts regarding improvements would be a great help.

I will give you a ring on Tuesday and look forward to speaking with you again.

Very truly yours,

Paul Richards

Paul Richards

A networking letter to an "influential person"

Dear Mr. Kearns:

As President of Mellon Bank and a person well known in financial circles, you have insight into many firms. That is the reason for this letter.

My most recent executive assignment has been as CFO of Carter Inc. In that position, my achievements contributed heavily to the following results:

— A major profit decline was reversed and our earnings have jumped 30%.

— A reorganization was put into effect and a new system was installed.

Earlier, I held several responsible positions with Henredon, a manufacturer of quality furniture.

Now, after careful thought, I have decided to seek out new opportunities in Pittsburgh. I know you are busy, but thought perhaps you could share my background with an associate who could benefit from my experience. CEOs or board members of consumer product manufacturers would be logical possibilities.

With this in mind, I am including a link below to my personal website listing my credentials. Please feel free to forward it to others. Thank you in advance for your help.

With best regards,

Jonathan Smith

Jonathan Smith

Thanks to the Internet and personal marketing websites... networking just got a lot easier.

Recapping this chapter. Many people don't like to do traditional networking. But the Internet, social networking sites and personal marketing websites are making networking easier and faster than ever before. If you don't have a personal marketing website... try it. It works.

Quick action steps. JMAC makes it easy for people to identify and contact influential alumni, as well as executives in selected industries. On your own use directories to get this information. Also, join social networking sites and appropriate professional associations, and refer people frequently to your site. Follow the guidelines and adapt the letter examples to your situation.

"Reach high, for stars lie hidden in your soul."
—*Pamela Vaul Starr*

"If at first you don't succeed, try, try, try again."
—*W.E. Hickson*

If you are an executive, your next job may very likely be one that is created for you.

You can develop offers, even when no current openings exist. You simply need to present yourself as a solution to a problem.

14 You can create your next new job

You can get a job created for yourself... one that is shaped to your talents.

The higher you go as a professional or executive, the more likely that the next position you accept will actually be created for you. Or, the position will be a situation that is reshaped to fit your talents.

Keep in mind this simple thought. We all hire top people when we are persuaded that the benefits of having them on board will sufficiently outweigh the dollar cost.

You can get offers, even if no job openings are said to exist. You simply need to present yourself as a solution to a problem. The "create a job" approach is for executives who want a job tailored to their best abilities.

A few examples might include an executive who can develop new products for a company, a sales executive with contacts in particular markets or a general manager who can start up a division in a specific industry.

Aside from executives, the "create a job" approach can also be considered by anyone who may have difficulty winning offers through other means. This includes those who have a narrow market for their talents, people who wish to change industries, or those who have been unemployed for a while or who want to stay in a specific geographic or industry area.

In these situations, to win the job you want, you may have to create it by making an employer aware of your ability to make contributions.

The following pages will give you some guiding principles as you consider this approach. You must focus on small to medium sized firms, go directly to people with the authority to create jobs, have a clear benefit proposition, take strong initiatives in your first meetings, and stir the employer's imagination.

1 Target the right organizations

The first principle to understand is that to have your best chance at creating a job, your highest probability targets are likely to be small to medium sized companies. This includes firms that are growing rapidly, bringing out new products, forming new divisions, acquiring other companies or reorganizing.

These are the firms that need good people, often from other industries. They are free to move quickly. Large corporations are the least likely to respond to this approach. Budgets are usually allocated far in advance, and hiring practices tend to be relatively slow and methodical.

Of course, there are exceptions. All you need to do is assess your talents and contact the firms most likely to need you, regardless of their size. And if you know a market well or have talents in a particular function, just consider the industries where they would apply.

2 Reach the right decision makers...

The second principle involves your reaching the appropriate high level people. For example, you must be able to communicate directly with the person you would most likely work for, or that person's boss.

In small and medium sized companies, it would be someone at the senior vice presidential level or the president who would likely be involved. Entrepreneurs, of course, can create jobs. So can affluent individuals who often have large staffs and interests in many organizations. In a larger company, be sure to choose the person who has ultimate responsibility for the area in which you can contribute.

When selecting the person to contact, aim on the high side. If you're not sure who to contact, start with the president. When you make contact at this level, you must be ready to communicate a benefit proposition.

13% of all $100K+ job seekers have at one time gotten a job that was created or reshaped for them.

3 Prepare a brief description of benefits you can bring

The third principle is to get across your benefit proposition. It must be an accurate, concise and easily understood description of what you can do.

> *"Some years ago, I hired a football coach from a little known California university. The only reason I saw him was that he wrote such a good letter outlining what he thought he could do for us."—owner, NFL football team*

Your message has to hold the promise of tangible value on a scale large enough to warrant an investment in you. In that initial communication, you will also need to establish your credentials. Mention specific results you achieved in the past. They are the best indicators of what you can do in the future.

If you're a VP Finance, you will obviously want to talk about how you can save money by cutting expenses. But if you want someone to get interested enough to create a job for you, you'll stand a much better chance if you cite tangible results.

For example, your cost cutting efforts led directly to a 5% increase in profits for your present employer; or your studies showed the firm was losing a million dollars a year on three product lines they could easily drop.

When you hold out the promise for potential benefits of that size, it is obvious to the reader that you might well be worth the investment.

Likewise, if you've developed many successful products, that is all well and good. However, if you expect someone to create a job, you'll stand a much better chance if you can state that you spearheaded development of three products now representing 20% of sales or that one now commands a 40% market share.

Achievements don't have to be large, but they do have to be significant. For instance, if you are an administrative executive, you might state that you managed a smooth introduction of new systems that lifted productivity 40%.

One key point to remember is that if you have an exciting idea to communicate, it may help if you can show how someone else has already used that idea successfully.

Dealing with opportunities is a key job for many executives. Most don't have enough time in the day and are predisposed to positive news from people who can help them. They will want to believe your message, so all you need do is make sure you provide positive reinforcement.

By the way, you can get your message across by phone or with a letter. Either way, make sure your "benefit proposition" is clear, easy to measure and significant; and be prepared to quickly establish your credentials.

4 Take strong initiatives in your first interview

The fourth principle is to take strong initiatives in your first interview. Remember, your initial communication held out the promise of a benefit. What are your ideas? Why do you think they'll work? Do you understand the company's problems and opportunities?

Address these areas, but always remember to convey humility. Acknowledge that the interviewer has a better grasp of the problems facing the company than you could possibly have; this will help build positive rapport. There are any number of simple phrases you might use. For example, you might say:

> *"I hope you didn't find my letter too presumptuous. No doubt you've already given a lot of consideration to these areas." Or…"I took a calculated risk in telling you I could cut manufacturing costs. I recognize that every company is unique, and what works well in one may not work so easily in another." Or… "I'm sure you've talked to many people who thought they knew your business better than you do. I don't mean to come across that way. I have a number of ideas, but let me first pay you the courtesy of listening to your opinion on these areas."*

No job is ever created out of thin air. You have to surface the need that is already in the back of someone's mind. Your conviction, passion and belief in the benefits you bring make the sale.

Comments like these set the stage for a cordial exchange of ideas. They can allow you to do the three things you need to accomplish in your first meeting: learn what the employer really wants, build rapport and focus the employer's attention on the areas where you can help.

Your first goal is to find out how the employer views the problem. What does he see as the key challenges? What is the "hot button"? What are the priorities as the employer sees them? Have attempts been made in the past? And how much progress has already been made? By asking a few questions and listening carefully, you will find out what the employer really wants. You will also be building rapport. Make sure you maintain a balanced conversation. Ask questions and make positive comments in response to the interviewer's remarks.

Most important, try to get the employer to share his innermost thoughts. Try to surface his vision for the organization. Only when he starts to think about this and the significant achievements he might realize, would he consider the possibility of creating a job.

If you are able to accomplish the above in the first interview, that is enough. State that you would like to give things some further thought and then clarify the benefits you might bring to the situation.

Show your enthusiasm and get agreement that a second interview would be worthwhile. If you've done these things, you're well on your way to having a job created for you. Remember, in your second interview you must reinforce your value by drawing an unusually clear picture of the benefits you can bring. Then you need to build enough enthusiasm to get an offer or be asked to speak with others.

5 Genuinely stir the employer's imagination

The fifth overall principle involves your need to stir the employer's imagination. The employer should begin to anticipate specific benefits and be able to relate them directly to your talents. The entire focus of the conversation should be on the future, with the employer picturing a company already benefiting from your contributions.

"It was very rare. But any decision we made to create a job was as much emotional as it was intellectual."
—*Former SVP, AT&T*

A dry recitation of proposed improvements won't be enough. You will have to convey enthusiasm and create a sense of excitement. Of course, to do this you will have to refine your thinking, clearly identifying those areas the employer sees as most important.

For each of them, be ready to discuss general approaches you would take to reinforce the notion that you will succeed. Your best way to do this is to tell stories about your past achievements.

If you build sufficient enthusiasm, the employer may conclude the meeting with a statement that he'd like to create a job for you. Or, he may ask you to meet with others in the company. If that happens, take the opportunity to build additional enthusiasm with every member of the team.

Keep in mind that if you're not getting interest, you might try the "report option." Here you need to make an offer to study the situation in more detail, perhaps to observe the company's operations or talk to knowledgeable outsiders, then to come back with a written report. The purpose? To make the entire subject more significant in the employer's mind.

"It is the same principle used by management consultants, advertising agencies, top sales producers, and others when they want to stimulate a company to action. The very act of a study, and the presentation of a report following it, builds an aura of importance. Your report doesn't need to be lengthy, and it doesn't have to require a great deal of work." —*SVP HR with a major advertising agency*

The report should, however, discuss areas where you would hope to make significant contributions. For each area, you would want to point out how you would proceed, demonstrating near term benefits for the company. If you get interesting input from outsiders or cite examples that support your points, it will make your presentation more compelling.

If you try the report option, be sure to stage it properly. Let the employer think it's important and ask for adequate time to present your findings. Your report, of course, would include a recommendation that a job be created. If the report is well received, you will have succeeded in creating a job.

What some people say

■ *"I am with General Foods. Creating jobs in our firm is rare. But our top executives do bring in people, and their decisions are as much emotional as intellectual. Also, when they have some-one lined up for a new job, it's a way for them to get their added budget requests through quickly."*

■ *"I met a friend at the annual meeting of a charity. One thing led to another, and my ideas on the future of his company got him interested. They created a role for me that I had a major part in shaping."*

■ *"Getting a job created takes longer. In fact, it took six discus-sions for the job I eventually accepted. But the position you get is really shaped to your talents and what you can bring to the table. These jobs are the most rewarding. The job I accepted was VP Operations of a new division."*

■ *"This was the third time I have made a career move, and each time a position was created for me. I think that having a website also made it easier this time around."*

Top executives create jobs when they discover the right person.

Recapping this chapter. The higher you go on the executive ladder, the more likely your next job will be created for you. It's all about presenting yourself as a "solution" to an employer's need or problem. Executives in small to medium-sized firms are the ones most likely to create jobs to bring you aboard.

Quick action steps. Make a list of all benefits you bring to an employer. And, make note of any contributions you are especially well equipped to provide, blending your skills, experience and knowledge. Follow the principles outlined, and make sure your contact comes across as highly personalized.

In our 2009 survey of 100,000 job seekers, 13% of professionals above $100K said they had gotten at least one job that was created or reshaped for them.

When you're comfortable using the phone, you'll get a lot more interviews.

Effective use of the phone is easy. You should use it aggressively to get in touch with top executives who can help.

15 Use the phone to achieve fast results

Power your marketing with telephone dynamics.

This can be a fast way to get the right interviews, and using the phone is easier than you think. Of course, some people are totally confident in their ability to use the phone. However, 90% of all job seekers are reluctant to make a "cold call."

Believe it or not, it's a mostly friendly and helpful world out there. Most executives are courteous and polite and go out of their way to project a good image of themselves and their company. The same holds true for others such as secretaries or administrative assistants.

Still, there is a certain misconception that all secretaries and assistants will always keep you from speaking with their bosses. They do screen calls, but it is part of their job to make sure that contact is made when appropriate.

> We estimate that about 12% of all job seekers really use the phone effectively. Only 5% use it to get interviews.

Using the phone to set interviews is especially important if you are in a small or mid-sized population area... a market not generally considered to be in the country's top 100 markets. It's easy to target your best prospects, and you just need to get into action. And, don't be deterred if your first call doesn't get you in the door. If it is a company you would really like to join, just call other executives in the organization.

Proven telephone guidelines that work

■ Standing will give you a power assist.

■ Do your phone work in batches. You need only one success each time to sustain your morale.

■ Make sure you know how you will be answering your phone. List questions you may be asked and write out the answers.

■ Prepare a 30 second commercial of your most important selling points. Rehearse it. Tape it and critique it.

■ One of the best times to reach executives is before 7:30 a.m. or after 5:30 p.m. Use their directories to go direct.

■ Smile while speaking over the phone and your voice will sound more pleasant. Be friendly, enthusiastic and positive.

■ Project a natural, confident tone—as you would when talking with a friend. Lower your voice. Speak slowly.

■ Be prepared for rejection. This is a numbers game. You can easily make 15 calls an hour.

■ Be sure your phone is answered properly. No clever answering machine messages.

■ The screener doesn't know who you are or your purpose. Focus on advice and information. No one has a reason to shy away from you. When speaking with the screener, get her name and use it. Be confident, positive and polite.

■ When following up, do not discuss your business other than to say the executive is expecting your call. Or use your job title.

■ If you begin to generate interest, do not reveal too much of your story. Remember, you want to press only for an interview, and it should be a request for just 20 minutes, even if it ends up being much longer.

Approaches for opening your conversations

The "good news" approach. Here you build a positive relationship based on specific "good news." Everyone likes to have good things happen and to hear from others who are enthusiastic about their good fortune. You can be sure that your message will immediately help to build a feeling of friendliness and warmth over the phone. This kind of approach can play an important role in winning extra interviews and getting people to help you.

The "third-party" approach. If you mention the name of a third party who knows the person you're calling, it helps to establish rapport, but it's also helpful even when they don't know each other. The approach is simple. It might go like this: *"Bill Regan, a partner with Ernst & Young, thought I should get in touch with you. He felt your growth not only suggests a good investment but might indicate a good employment possibility. His insights prompted me to follow up with you personally. Do you have a moment?"*

The "specific reason" approach. Anyone who has experience in getting things done can consider using this "specific reason" approach. It's straightforward and can go like this: *"Mr. Franklin, I have a 'specific reason' for calling you. I know the line of business you are in and something of the processes you use. During the past 15 months, I have been able to save a company like yours approximately $850,000. I would like to share the details with you. Does your calendar permit a meeting later this week?"*

"Perhaps you can help me" approach. If a specific opening has already been filled, someone can help you meet a hiring official in another part of the company. If the individual you contact does not have a precise fit in his department, perhaps he could help you meet a person in another division. If you are told that the person you want to speak to is out, the best response is, *"Thanks. Perhaps you can help me. When is a good time to call back?"*

Tips for handling people who screen your call

■ As previously mentioned, start by using the name of the person who is the "screener." Once a person knows he or she has been identified, their manner will become more personal.

■ When asked your name, identify yourself with an organization if possible. If you don't get through on your first attempt, and you can't get a suitable time to call back, suggest a time when you will call the screener back, don't leave a message.

■ When you call back, use the screener's name with the receptionist. Try this procedure: *"Since he (or she) is so hard to reach, would you do me a small favor? May I call back to see if he would be interested in speaking with me for a few minutes?"* If you must leave a message, leave one of potential benefit.

■ Consider reversing your attempt to speak with the decision maker by asking for an internal referral to another line manager in the area in which you might want to work for the company.

■ If the screener refers you to HR, get the name of the person to whom you will be speaking. Call back later for that person or request a transfer to the person you are looking for.

■ After a few minutes of discussion, ask two or three penetrating questions about the company's needs. When asked difficult questions, those who don't know the answer are more inclined to refer you to an appropriate line manager.

■ After a few days, you can also call back the screener and explain that while the personnel people were helpful, they were not really able to answer the questions you had in mind.

■ You may encounter the question: *"Are you looking for a job?"* The answer might be: *"Yes, I am; do you think you could help me? Though I'm employed, a friend suggested your firm to me."*

■ Or, you may encounter the comment, *"We don't have any openings at the present time."* The response: *"I appreciate a person who is direct; however, I have such a strong interest in the firm. I really believe that with your recent growth, I could be a great asset. Will you allow me to tell you why?"*

Some openers for after you reach the right person

■ Considering what is happening to the technology of our business, I know I can be very useful to you because of my training and experience in _____.

■ From your annual report, I read that the company's expanding in the _____ area. That's an area where I could help, and I'd like to schedule an appointment.

■ My friend _____ suggested that I make a point of contacting you. You may recall from my letter that I have experience in _____ that might be of help to you.

■ With my background in _____ and the recent news about _____, I thought it would be a good idea to get in touch with you. Could you suggest a convenient time? Do you have 20 minutes before you get started some morning next week?

■ Mr. _____, your company has a tremendous reputation for marketing leading products. I'd like very much to visit with you to explain how I could contribute to that reputation through my work in _____. Do you have a half hour free this Tuesday?

How you can turn rejection into an interview

Less than 1% of all job hunters ever follow up a rejection letter. Follow-up requires a special tenacity, a certain "thickness of skin," and an ability to accept rejection as a challenge. A person who has arrived at the perfect company and met with rejection should be prepared to do the following.

Find out all about the firm from every source available; call, write, visit, speak to as many people as necessary; go through third-party channels; and depart from conventional approaches. Here are three approaches that might fit your circumstance.

"Acting puzzled & helpless"

This does not call for much acting ability for many of us, because it is the way we feel when we receive those politely worded notes that give us the bad news that our services are not required. We are puzzled because we cannot understand how they can't recognize our qualities, and we are helpless to do much about it.

One way to follow up is to call and thank the sender of the letter for their reply. Then try to engage them in a frank discussion about your failure to understand what is going on. The usual explanation is that there are no vacancies available at the present time.

However, you must not let this reply end the conversation. You must try to keep it going. What almost everyone in a job search needs is a preliminary, non-obligatory talk with a person who is qualified to explain what the company does and how it goes about meeting its employment needs.

This is what you should ask for, because as a puzzled and helpless person, you do not know what to do next. Here is how this might work.

"Mr. Jones, I got your letter this morning and it tells me that you are going to keep my resume on file against further openings. I'm a bit puzzled at that because I only sent a short note to the company suggesting a meeting to talk about what I might be able to do for you."

This must be delivered without a trace of sarcasm because that could kill your relationship. Then, keep quiet and see what the answer may be. Silence is powerful. Carrying on from here, find out how the organization goes about recruiting. People enjoy giving advice, especially when sincerely asked by someone who really needs it. For example, you might ask... *does the company ever employ people with my disciplines and experience? Do they advertise jobs, or do they place people in the company from other sources? If so, which recruiters do they use?*

These questions are asked because you do not know the answers, not because you are trying to be "smart." There is still enough warm feeling in even the most harassed executive for you to get some very useful information from them. What you are seeking is specific information, such as the names of heads of departments, plans for expansion, ideas for approaching personalities, the real "stuff" that the company is made of. With that information you can then approach someone else or keep it on file for follow-up next month.

"I need your understanding"

This approach is straightforward.
It's about asking some direct questions.

Was it correct to send my letter to the president in the first place? Does the Personnel Department really handle recruitment at my level and in my discipline? It is important for me to know this, because I may well have approached the company incorrectly.

How should I go about reaching the right decision maker?

A young person should request information or assistance in reaching the right person by talking with lower levels of management. Executives should get into the upper levels by asking who handles specific responsibilities. Here's another example:

Mary, I need your help and I can sense that you would like to help me if you could. But what I must find out is this: how do I get to talk to Harry Smith for a few minutes at a time when he can listen to me or arrange to meet me? Charm is the watchword. Patience in building relationships, careful listening and projecting a positive attitude will all help create a warm response.

"Acting very assertive"

Mary, I was surprised to learn this morning that you had sent my letter addressed to Mr. Jones to your Personnel Department. What happened? My note simply suggested a meeting with Mr. Jones. By now it may be all over the company that I am looking for a job.

This could sound too strong if not said with a smile. If you don't get the response you need, go on. For example... *What we ought to do is this: I need your help to recover the letter from Personnel and have Mr. Jones look at it himself. Obviously, he is the man I must see. Can we do something about that?*

Should I write to him again and mention what has happened? Perhaps I could send you a copy with a note to give it to him? Another way of using this style is to say... *I must speak to Mr. Jones right away, Mary. This is serious. Someone has sent a confidential letter that I addressed to him to other people in your organization, and that worries me very much.* This frequently makes the breakthrough, so be ready with your telephone script for him or her.

Anyone can learn to be powerful on the phone. So, why not use the phone to set interviews?

Recapping this chapter. Take full advantage of what the phone can mean for you. Setting interviews via the phone is important for people in small or mid-sized population areas... markets not in the top 100.

Quick action steps. Choose the principles you feel comfortable with and role play them out loud. Make notations on small index cards to use as prompts when on the phone. If the wording you try doesn't work, compose something different for next time.

"A little more persistence, a little more effort, in what seems like hopeless failure, may turn to glorious success."
— *Albert Hubbard*

"Success seems to be largely a matter of hanging on after others have let go." —*William Feather*

"Clear your mind of can't." —*Dr. Samuel Johnson*

Some think of interviews as an interrogation.
It should be a meeting of peers... and much more.

To come out number one among five to ten other finalists requires some personal skills and a well thought out presentation.

16 Making sure you interview at your very best

Use these seven proven rules for interviewing success.

1 Find out what's most important to the interviewer

Ask questions that will get interviewers to articulate what's most important. Of course, you'll need to find out what happened to the last person in the job. Ask about his experiences and those of his superiors. Find out to whom the position reports and how long that person was in the job. Ask... *"What would be the biggest challenge I would face?"* Find out how the interviewer sees the problem, what the expectations are and what progress has been made. Of course, once you find out what's most important to the firm... you need to tell them that you have what they want. Too many people let their resume be the basis for the whole discussion.

2 Tell stories that make people remember you

In these stories indicate positive things you did to help organizations. The idea is to show how you demonstrated a particular skill or a personal quality.

Develop SOAR stories that cover situations where you can demonstrate the value of fresh thinking as a means to improve productivity or solve problems. Employers need to feel that you are the answer to one of their problems. If you can show them how you met or exceeded the needs in other places, they may conclude that you can do the same for them.

The idea is to create stories that demonstrate the benefits you bring. Remember, your "tickets" alone (degrees, titles, etc.) will not necessarily motivate another employer to hire you. You must use *action words* and *phrases* that add interest beyond your credentials. In the final analysis, employers hire people for what those phrases imply.

3 Surface and deal with any objections that arise

Your next key to interviewing is to be able to overcome objections in a smooth and seamless way. With today's competition, if you stumble, there are too many others the employer can turn to. So, why play this by ear? Here is a simple method for handling objections, the "ARTS method." The letters stand for the following:

A = Acknowledge the objection.
R = Redirect the person's concern.
T = Test to be sure you've removed the concern.
S = Use a story to make your point.

Whenever someone raises an objection, the tension level rises. In step A reduce the tension level.

A = Acknowledge the objection

"I can understand your concern, and I would like to address it for you." Or *"You've raised an interesting point. It deserves some frank discussion."* The phrases are not so important—it's the feeling you impart. You have acted in a reassuring way; it's clear that you feel secure about your abilities.

R = Redirect their concern

Let's say the interviewer raised the fact that your experience was in a different industry. *"What qualities are you looking for in an ideal candidate that prompted this concern?"* Now, you can't change your past, but you can show that you are someone who contributes quickly (e.g., *"When you raise that question, I understand that you want to be sure the person you put in this job is someone who will contribute quickly. Isn't that it?"*) The interviewer will reaffirm that you are indeed correct. With just a little thought, it is easy to refocus the conversation toward the positive qualities that are really on the interviewer's mind.

T = Use a testing question

The idea is to see if you removed their concern. Here is an example of asking a testing question: *"If I could show that I could contribute quickly, even when learning new information, would that help?"*

After you get a positive response, you can go directly to your answer, or you can introduce one of your key strengths. You might say: *"If I could show you that I work well under pressure, might that ease your concern somewhat?"*

S = Use a supporting story to confirm

The final thing is to use a supporting story. Remember, what really counts is the fact that you did not get flustered. If you've done it right, interviewers won't be that concerned about your exact answer. They'll be thinking, *"This person handled that situation very well."* Note: An objection is really a sign of interest. If employers were not interested, they would not bother asking you to overcome the objection.

4 Answer questions seamlessly and with confidence

If you want to be at your best, be sure to have answers prepared to these common questions.

- *Why did you join your present firm?*
- *Why are you leaving?*
- *Why have you stayed so long?*
- *What's wrong with your present firm?*
- *Have you managed people before?*

- *What are your capabilities that will help us?*
- *What major challenges have you faced?*
- *Have you fired people before?*
- *What references can you give us?*
- *Does your employer know you are looking?*

- *Describe a typical day in your job.*
- *What areas of your job do you enjoy the most?*
- *Which jobs have you enjoyed the most? Why?*
- *How well do you handle pressure?*
- *What do you look for when you hire people?*

- *How does the firm view your performance?*
- *Which areas of your work have been criticized?*
- *What do you think of your ex-boss?*
- *Why haven't you found a job so far?*
- *Can you fit into an unstructured environment?*

- *Why do you want to work for us?*
- *What are your greatest accomplishments?*
- *Describe your management style.*
- *How effective are you as a motivator?*
- *What decisions do you delegate?*

- *What types of controls do you use?*
- *What is your biggest strength? Weakness?*
- *Would you classify yourself as a leader?*
- *How do you handle confrontation?*
- *How often have you had raises?*

- *What do you think you are worth?*
- *Why aren't you earning more at your age?*
- *What would you like to be earning in two years?*
- *What were your highest earnings?*
- *What are the key reasons for your success?*

- *Who are your closest friends? What do they do?*
- *Are you confident about addressing a group?*
- *How would a friend describe you?*
- *What types of problems do you struggle with?*
- *Are you active in your community?*

- *Are you interested in sports?*
- *Have you ever been arrested or convicted?*
- *How good is your health?*
- *How do you spend your spare time? Your hobbies?*
- *What was the last book you read?*

- *Have you been refused a bond? Been bankrupt?*
- *In what areas can you improve yourself?*
- *Tell me about yourself.*
- *What is your view of the political climate?*
- *How strong is your financial situation?*

- *What people do you admire?*
- *What kind of work environment are you looking for?*
- *Where else are you interviewing?*
- *Other offers received?*

- *If you started over, what would you do differently?*
- *How would others describe your work ethic?*

Sample answers to common questions

What is your biggest weakness?

"Well, I really don't feel I have any major weaknesses that affect my working ability. At times I have a tendency to be impatient about getting things done."

Why are you leaving?

"I want to earn more, have added responsibility, and expand my knowledge in my field. These opportunities don't exist in my present firm."

With no industry experience, could you contribute?

"I expect to be able to contribute in a short time. Obviously, it will take some time to get my feet wet. However, there are a number of things I have accomplished before, and I may be able to institute some of them once I gain a better understanding of your firm. I'm a quick learner." Support your claim with a SOAR story.

How long would you stay with us?

"I'm looking for a career. However, I'm a realist. If I don't do the job, you won't want me around; and if there is no opportunity, it won't be right for me."

What's wrong with your current firm?

"I don't feel there is anything wrong with the firm. I have enjoyed working there, and they have some really top people. It's a good company, but I am ready for some added responsibility and challenge."

What are your short range objectives?

Keep your answer focused on the job for which you are interviewing. It is not in your best interest to pick short range objectives that the job or company might be unable to provide.

What are your long range objectives?

In dealing with this question, it is a good idea to remain flexible. A brief answer that refers to moving up the ladder as quickly and as far as your capabilities permit will suffice.

How good is your health?

Besides saying your health is fine, you should go on to state that you are accustomed to working long hours and are quite capable of keeping up a fast pace. If you have a health problem that the interviewer could find out about, give a truthful answer. However, point out that your condition has had no adverse effect on performance, attendance or ability to give 100%.

If you started over, what would you do differently?

"On the whole I would have to say that I am extremely proud of my career achievements and quite happy with my career progression to date."

What do you think of your boss?

If you think your boss is great, it is pretty easy to answer this question. On the other hand, if you really didn't get along with your boss, then this question becomes challenging. Never discuss the shortcomings of your boss. Doing so will make you sound like a whiner or troublemaker. Instead, comment briefly on some positive aspects of your boss, be they in his personality or her management style… and leave it at that.

Why haven't you found a job so far?

Being apologetic or simply saying that it's a tough market in your field will not help you. Depending upon the length of your unemployment, it may be enough to respond that you are not seeking a job, but are selectively looking for the right career opportunity and have not yet found it.

What was the last book you read, movie you saw, or sporting event you attended?

Unless the movie or book is controversial, tell the truth. But, it's important that you have read, seen, or attended whatever you claimed, since more detailed questioning may follow.

What's your major accomplishment in your last job?

Pick those that seem to line up well with the major elements of the position. For example, if you have accomplishments in both cost and general accounting, and you're interviewing for a general accounting position, you obviously want to bias your answer toward the position for which you are a candidate. The goal is to always show the interviewer that your accomplishments line up with the company needs.

What interests you most about our position?... the least?

The response to the former should be an aspect or aspects of the job that benefit the employer, not you. For example, you might cite the challenge of the problems to be solved, or the opportunity to apply your skills to particular challenges. For the second question, you might say, *"At this point I have not heard anything about the job that turns me off."*

Why aren't you earning more at your age?

If you are in a low paying industry, make sure that you point out that you have received performance raises. Also point out that your industry / function is traditionally low paying, which is one of the reasons you are looking for a new job.

When discussing how much you are making, respond in terms of value of the job. For example, *"My position has a range that goes from _____ to _____, and I am well over the midpoint. Because of performance, I'm one of the better paid in the firm."*

What do your subordinates think of you?

This is an opportunity for you to sell yourself through another person's viewpoint. Offer strengths and attributes that are relevant to your ability to perform well in the position for which you're being considered.

Why do you want to work for us?

If this question is asked very early in the interview, you may not really have a good answer. Therefore, give a response instead like this:

"Based on what I learned about your organization from people I know, I did some research and found that you've achieved impressive sales increases for the last six quarters. Given that kind of growth, I felt that my strong background in _____ might be valuable to you."

People often decide if they like you in the first
5 minutes. Then, you've got to keep it going.
A good way to overcome objections is to bring them
up and minimize them during your presentation.

5 Read the interviewer and adjust your behavior

Wouldn't it be nice to be able to *"read"* everyone who interviews you... and based on their personality and behavior, know the kind of candidate they prefer?

To influence the person interviewing you, we have found that you will do best if you can match the style of that person. Most people's personality can be gauged on four levels. Where you and your interviewer fit on personality measurements will affect how well you connect with each other. You want to judge where someone sitting on the other side of the table likely fits.

The "very strong" interviewer. *The degree to which a person is a very strong person... reflects their need to be in control... their* need to direct and dominate. Someone who is very strong is often demanding, forceful and competitive.

This person may maintain a cool or closed posture. Many top executives are high on the scale of being "very strong." When they question you, they focus on "what you did"... the actions you took... rather than "why" you took them. They will be looking for someone who is bottom-line in their orientation. They prefer others who are brief, to the point, and decisive like they are. They often make hiring decisions quickly, and prefer those who seem efficient and goal oriented.

The "highly social" interviewer. *The degree to which a person is highly social reflects their need to be involved with people* and influence them. Someone who is highly social is often persuasive, enthusiastic and friendly. These people are often animated and express their feelings quite readily. They tend to adopt an open posture and are warm by their nature. They will be looking for how you managed people, who you worked with in getting consensus and making your decisions. They will be much less likely to concern themselves with "what" you did, or "why" you did something.

Chances are this person will prefer people like themselves... expressive and sociable. They will focus on how interesting you are, and will enjoy testimonials and war stories. They usually put a priority on people skills and are likely to make hiring decisions based upon emotions or gut feel.

The "highly service oriented" interviewer. *The degree to which a person is highly service oriented reflects their preference for structure...* situations that are stable and steady. Someone who is very service oriented is often loyal, predictable and patient.

These people tend to be relaxed and warm. They express their feelings and are more casual and open. When they question you, their focus may be on "why" you did something rather than "what" you did. They will be focusing on service to the company, and looking for people who project steadiness. These people often make hiring decisions in a deliberate manner and like to be assured of a person's stability. They dislike unpredictable people whose opinions might represent any form of conflict.

The "highly cautious" interviewer. *The degree to which a person is highly cautious reflects their preference for procedures and order,* environments that allow a cautious, systematic approach to solving problems. Highly cautious people are often conventional, accurate and restrained.

These people may adopt a closed posture and be more formal in their questioning. They too will focus on "why you did something"... trying to analyze your response. They usually put a priority on product or service quality and analytical decision-making.

This individual will respond best to you if you demonstrate you are conscientious, accurate, and analytical in your approach to problem solving. This type of person will disapprove of you if you appear to be disorganized, or are unclear when answering questions. They believe in making hiring decisions in an analytical way. Many HR executives are risk-averse and don't want to make a mistake.

It only stands to reason that if you can get an accurate reading on the person who might be responsible for selecting you over others... you will be better able to control the situation and project your image in best keeping with their likely preferences.

Only 7 to 9% of all job seekers are well prepared for interviewing. By learning and using the advice in this chapter, you can get a great advantage.

When a company is interviewing different people—it's about individual competition. Be at your very best. If you've done your homework and are prepared, it will clearly be evident to the people who interview you.

6 Develop positive chemistry right at the start

Are interviews just question-and-answer sessions? This may happen, but an interview that turns into a good offer involves far more. Last year there were more than 800 million interviews, and no two were the same.

So how do you prepare? Compare this to a sports contest— there were millions of them and none were the same. In an interview or a contest, you can't plan exactly how things will go, but you can have a game plan for coming out on top. We guide clients in achieving personal chemistry with executives of all personalities. Here are some ways to make sure that you build maximum chemistry with everyone.

Build chemistry by researching the firm and being informed

Did you ever meet a person for the first time who knew a lot about you? It takes you by surprise, doesn't it? It's a great way to make a positive first impression. One friend of mine, an attorney, attributes his success to research he does ahead of time.

Four out of every five of his clients tell him that he wins their business because he knows a lot more about them than anyone else. When you arrange an appointment, use the opportunity to gather more information. Many people have been able to get job descriptions and brochures ahead of time by requesting them over the phone. Visit the firm's website, but go further to learn about their industry and the person you will be meeting.

Build chemistry by impressing the front office staff

Building chemistry with the front office staff can also make a difference. Can you guess what percentage of executives say their secretaries influence them? One-third? One-half? Well, about two-thirds of them do. Not too long ago, I was interrupted by Carol, who stated that Mr. Baxter had arrived for his interview.

I had forgotten about the appointment, and it was a busy day. I immediately asked, *"What do you think of him, Carol?"* She didn't say a word. She just gave a thumbs-down signal.

That was the end for poor Baxter. No one ever taught him how important it is to make a positive impression on the front office staff. I told Carol to have him see one of our assistants, and to provide her opinion first. So, please be attentive to the front office staff.

Build chemistry by projecting the right image

When we are on the hiring end, many of us reach a negative decision in just a few minutes. Why? Well, if you have the credentials, you establish a good initial impression or you don't. And what determines chemistry? People silently react to the image you project, your dress, your posture and body language, the things you say about any subject, and the way you answer questions. Each of us is continually projecting some kind of image. It isn't just physical or dress either, although your appearance speaks before you say a word. It's also a matter of attitude and enthusiasm, and whether you project integrity.

Build chemistry by paying compliments

Do you like compliments? Do you think others do? You bet they do. So before the interview, read or talk to people about the firm and uncover good things to say. Let the interviewer know you heard them.

You can compliment their facilities, people, ads or many other things. However, be specific. Don't just say that people you know are impressed by their product. Talk about why they are impressed. All of us like to hear about how our products have pleased customers. By giving details, you show you have given the subject some thought, and that your compliment is not just empty flattery. Mark Twain once said, *"I can live for two months on a good compliment."*

Build chemistry by asking questions

Ideally, you should ask questions for a good portion of every interview. This enables you to assert some control and reduces interviewing pressure. The way you ask questions and the specific nature of their content will tell a lot about you. For this reason, we want each of our clients to have a questioning strategy. By asking intelligent questions, you will build your image in the eyes of the interviewer—and you will be building chemistry. You want him thinking, "Certainly, John seems very sharp, well informed... impressive." Of course, among the key questions you ask should be ones that are designed to find out what is "wrong" with the job or the company.

You might consider these "offensive questions" as opposed to "defensive questions" when you are fielding the answers. The point to keep in mind is that they need to be questions that, from the perspective of the interviewer, will get right to the heart of what is going on in the organization.

Types of questions you might ask

▪ Does the CEO have strong convictions about the approach needed to meet your goals?

▪ How closely do R & D and sales work together?

▪ If I were to become VP, how much input would you expect on selecting new products?

▪ Do you have a strong team in place, or will you expect me to recruit my own team?

▪ You need to have new capabilities to achieve your goals. Would I be given a free hand to do that, or would that cause political problems?

▪ Is top management unanimous on the need to develop new lines quickly?

▪ Would you see the major thrust as positioning the firm for a public offering... or a merger?

▪ Given you are #3 in your market right now, what is the timetable for improving your future?

Build chemistry by the way you answer questions

Keep in mind that the interviewer wants someone who can do the job, and wants to find that person in a minimum of time. The *way* you answer questions has more to do with building chemistry than *what* you say. For example, how do you handle the number one question in interviewing: *"Tell me about yourself."*

You'll want to answer, but chances are you're not sure what they want to hear. You could start out by talking about the kind of person you are and some of your attributes, but that may not be what the interviewer is interested in. Faced with such a dilemma, a safe way out is to self-qualify your answer: *"Charles, I'd be happy to tell you about myself, and I'm sure you are interested in my work experience. I'll focus on the past few years and how they relate to your position. I can start with my most recent experience if you like."*

When you self-qualify, you give the interviewer an opportunity to respond, and to direct the conversation to another area. That way, you can avoid talking for ten minutes about the wrong things. Be prepared and have your own 60- to 120-second commercial ready.

When you answer questions, gear your comments to potential contributions related to sales, profits, cost reduction, innovations, etc. When there is a silence, make sure you have prepared some questions in advance. Create an opportunity to demonstrate knowledge. Being prepared builds confidence and allows you to be more spontaneous. Always maintain eye contact, and establish your sincerity and integrity.

When you encounter difficult questions, use the "U-turn" technique. For example, *"You look very impressive on paper, Marge. If you're this good, you ought to be able to solve all of our problems. Tell me, why we should hire you?"*

Now, of course, you know the person doesn't believe you're that good. However, if you begin to talk about why they should hire you, you run the real risk of going on about all the wrong things. With the "U-turn" technique, you don't give an answer. Instead, turn the question around in a way that acknowledges the status of the interviewer and pays an indirect compliment.

For example: *"I have a lot of experience I think you could use. But it would be presumptuous of me to tell you what you need before I've shown the courtesy of listening to what you think the priorities are. If you'd be kind enough to share some of your thoughts on them, perhaps I could give a more intelligent answer."*

Comments on chemistry
"Most of my interviews were with medium-sized firms in Arizona. Their selection processes were heavy on personal fit, chemistry with others and attitude."

■ *"Chemistry is where it's at. When it's down to a few candidates, competency rarely is the issue."*

■ *"Obviously, connecting to openings is important, but in the final stages, working at building chemistry with everyone you meet is just as important."*

7 Dress for success. Your image speaks for you before you say a word.

Guidelines for women

Clothes tell the employer how you see yourself. Your hairstyle and your choice of makeup is either going to reinforce or detract from your professional image. The accessories you choose—shoes, purse, jewelry—make a further statement about your awareness of that image. There is no single look for all women. Guidelines about dress have become more flexible. "Presence" involves not only appearance, but also self-confidence and knowledge. Here are some guidelines.

"Fashions change but style is forever."   —*Georgio Armani*

"Project elegance and you'll project success."   —*Valentino*

Hairstyle and makeup... nails and perfume

A good haircut is essential. Short to medium length hair is most appropriate. Keep away from an "extreme" look—anything frizzy, too full, teased or too long. Your makeup should appear natural.

If you have never worn makeup, recognize that most people feel their appearance can be enhanced by some foundation, a touch of blush, a light lipstick, and some mascara. Your nails should be medium length and filed attractively. No squares or points. Keep to an oval shape. Keep away from overly distracting shades, even though they may be fashionable at the time. If you are accustomed to wearing fragrance, don't use anything overpowering.

Clothing for interviews

A well tailored suit is always appropriate for an interview. When choosing colors, keep to an understated, conservative look. A solid color, a muted tweed or plaid, or a subtle pinstripe is always in good taste. You want your next employer to remember you, not your outfit.

If you generally wear bright or bold colors, choose a scarf or blouse in a shade you enjoy. Blouses or sweaters to go with your suit should either be white, off white, beige, or a color complementary to your suit.

A solid color dress, properly tailored and well fitting, is also appropriate for interviewing. A subtle plaid or stripe can also be correct. Since skirt lengths vary, select a length in keeping with the overall style of suit or dress you are wearing. Times change, and there are always exceptions, but a good rule of thumb is nothing shorter than an inch below your knee.

Shoes, stockings, briefcases and jewelry

Generally, stockings should be in a neutral shade, seamless, and snug fitting. Stockings in a complementary shade to your outfit are periodically in fashion and would also be acceptable. Stay away from heavily textured or patterned stockings. The leather of the shoes you select should be well polished. Keep away from clogs, sandals, and platform soled shoes.

If you plan to carry a briefcase, put your handbag items in it. Don't appear "laden down." Keep your jewelry simple. The key is never to use anything so startling that it detracts from the impression you want to make. Never wear a handful of rings.

Your general appearance

There is an unspoken "managerial" dress code for women. It is more tailored than feminine (no plunging necklines or sheer fabrics) and enhances a "power" look. These emphasize a woman's ability to perform on the job, rather than femininity. Make sure you look like you are ready for the income level to which you aspire. Body language is also important. Straight posture says that you take pride in your appearance.

Initial perceptions are difficult
to change… for better or worse.

Guidelines for men

Looking good means feeling good and feeling confident. Before you launch your search, assess your wardrobe. You need several outfits because you must expect to go through a series of two, three, or more interviews. Use your clothing to project a personality that fits the situation and the firm.

Suits and shirts

Most people will do best if their suits are properly fitted and conservative. One of the most difficult things for most men to do is throw away suits. The time for such action may be now.

Before you make a purchase, prepare for your fitting by deciding how you will wear the suit. Allow for nothing in the pockets except a few bills and some change. When interviewing, your wallet can be kept in a briefcase.

Another important observation relates to the length of your jacket sleeve. Allow 5" from the top of your thumb to the end of your sleeve. Don't let tailors persuade you to take longer sleeves!

Clothing must fit properly. Go back at least twice for alterations. Allow for some slight shrinkage in dry cleaning. The front of your pants cuff should barely touch the shoe.

Regarding the fit of your shirt, if you have gained a significant amount of weight, you may be wearing your collar too tight. Ex-athletes who have trimmed down will often find that their collars have become loose.

Generally speaking, you will want to avoid short-sleeved shirts. Those who wear cuff links should make sure they are simple. A gaudy look is likely to be perceived as a negative.

Ties, shoes & accessories

Ties can be fun and can give you a unique look. To a great extent, this element of your wardrobe is a matter of preference. Above all, be sure your tie is clean. Bow ties do little to enhance most people's image.

Many people feel that shoes are a man's most important clothing item. This is because a person's appearance is immediately downgraded if he is wearing an unattractive pair of shoes.

A famous designer was recently quoted as saying, *"Whether a man is wearing relaxed, business or formal attire, you can assess him most quickly by the shoes and watch he is wearing."*

Your shoes should be well polished and light to medium in weight. Slip-ons are increasingly acceptable. The old military "spitshine" is still a real power builder.

Don't underrate accessories. Belts and belt buckles should be conservative. Socks should be over the calf in length and normally a solid color complementing the suit. It is not necessary to have a handkerchief nicked in your breast pocket, but it can be a nice touch.

A wallet and briefcase show a lot about a man. Thin wallets and neat briefcases are a nice complement to your overall appearance.

Your general appearance

As a rule, if you appear older than you would like, your hair should be on the short side. For most men in their 20s or 30s, however, a somewhat longer look is appropriate.

A clean shave is a must. For late afternoon interviews, carry an electric razor in your briefcase. As far as after-shave or cologne is concerned, keep it subtle. For those of you who are overweight, clothes can cover up just so much. Try to lose some extra pounds if possible. If not, stand up straight and sit tall. Obviously, you want to look your best at all times.

enthusiasm!

Show enthusiasm... with everyone you meet. Do this on the phone... in face-to-face interviews... and in your follow-up letters. Nothing is more important, and it helps create chemistry.

"Nothing great is ever achieved without enthusiasm."
— *Ralph Waldo Emerson*

"If you can give your son or daughter a gift, let it be enthusiasm."
—*Bruce Barton*

A classical follow-up letter to an interview

Dear Mr. Carson:

You're probably surprised to hear from me so quickly. But, I left your office with such enthusiasm that I felt compelled to mention some added thoughts.

First, let me thank you and your associates for a most interesting afternoon. Everything about Sigma Systems is professional, and I was very impressed. Second, I wanted to focus on your need for an action-oriented person who can produce short-term results, because I am confident I am that person. Consider my performance in the last two years.

Under my direction, operating costs were reduced by $2,000,000 and profit jumped by 121%. In addition, the above were achieved with a staff reduction of 8%.

There is no question that I can do at least as well for Sigma, if not better. Judging from your comments at our meeting, I suspect you agree.

The one concern you did express related to my financial needs. Over the years, I've learned that one major factor determines whether something is cheap or expensive. It's the marketplace that ultimately determines a person's value.

In this case, I believe that your first consideration is with the results I can deliver. I have to believe that the return to the company would be substantial. Thanks again for your time, and I hope you'll consider me for what I know is a great opportunity for both of us.

Sincerely,

Janet Wilson
Janet Wilson

Other basics for interviewing

■ Avoid arriving more than 7 minutes early. If kept waiting too long, explain that you have another appointment and ask for a time you can come back.

■ Never bring packages or unnecessary materials.

■ Always avoid smoking and take a cue on drinks.

■ Never read mail on your interviewer's desk.

■ Never drum your fingers, look at your watch or exhibit other signs that might reflect disinterest or boredom.

■ Avoid discussions on race, religion or politics. And don't provide responses that make you seem like a "yes-man."

■ Never be a braggart and don't exaggerate. Use "name dropping" sparingly... if at all. If you do name drop, you must be very smooth about it.

> ❝ 50% of all new hires are people who employers simply liked the best. ❞

■ If your liabilities are pointed out, never apologize for them.

■ Never say anything critical about your past employers or bosses. Never be negative.

■ Don't let an interview carry on too long. When a discussion peaks, diplomatically lead to an end of the meeting.

■ Never linger after an interview... or stay around the hallways of a company speaking with others.

■ Emphasize recent experiences, use recent stories and project diversified interests and a strong work ethic.

■ There will always be questions for which you won't have answers. Don't let it bother you.

■ Don't be controlling. Keep an eye on your interviewer's body language and your own.

■ Read between the lines. Find a way to answer questions that should have been asked, but were not.

■ Follow up every interview with an enthusiastic letter.

■ It's a bad sign if an interviewer accepts a number of phone calls. It's a signal that there may not be much interest or things are not going well.

■ It's a good sign if the interviewer does more talking than you, or if he asks or talks about you solving his problems.

How you interview is important. There are always many other candidates under consideration.

Recapping this chapter. Successful interviewing depends on finding out and reacting to what's most important to the interviewer. Tell stories that make people remember you... surface and deal with objections... answer questions with confidence, read people and build chemistry.

Quick action steps. Try to master the information provided, and follow the six proven rules. Have your SOAR stories prepared, as well as your approach for handling liabilities. For our clients, JMAC is a source for market intelligence on employers and industries before interviews. On your own, you can find other sources that can be accessed online.

"The secret to success in life is for man to be ready for his opportunity when it comes."   *—Benjamin Disraeli*

Most people simply assume that they are good at interviewing and take it for granted. That's a big mistake. And, many assume that negotiating is something they are automatically good at. That's a big mistake too.

Most people leave money on the negotiating tables.
Here is a formula approach to getting an initial offer raised, and perhaps negotiating a signing bonus or other "perks."

17 Use our 7-step negotiation formula

This formula is simple, straightforward and easy to use.

Since most people seldom face a personal negotiating experience, it should come as no surprise that few of us are real experts at negotiating for ourselves. While they may be excellent company negotiators, we have seen many strong people leave serious money on the table when it came to negotiating their own package.

Now, the first thing you need to decide... is when to start a negotiation process. Some people mistakenly think negotiation is a continuous selling situation that occurs throughout their interviews. However, before you ever attempt to negotiate, you have to make sure that the employer is "sold on you."

Once an offer has been presented, you can't negotiate unless there is some hope you can get the employer to offer new terms. You need to sense this on an individual basis. That's where negotiations begin.

> **“**Less than 3% of all professional and executive job seekers are prepared for negotiating.**”**

What to negotiate

Coming to grips with what should be negotiated is, of course, different for everyone. Not too long ago we handled a marketing executive from Kellogg in Michigan. His primary goal was to have his family move to a new area that met outdoor lifestyle requirements, and he started by suggesting to us that a 20% reduction in income would be acceptable.

However, after a three-month search, he accepted a top position in Boca Raton. When we finished helping with his negotiations, his compensation ended up 15% higher, and he received a signing bonus, as well.

Another executive was with J & J. He wanted out of the major corporate environment. He left his large company career behind when he landed with a venture capital group. His assignment was to oversee ventures that the firm funded by serving as acting CEO. He was to complete the initial setup, find a permanent

CEO, and then move on to another assignment, but remain on the board. Based in Castle Pines, Colorado, he will handle two ventures simultaneously for six-month periods—eight over two years. His base of $200,000 was a decrease, but if just one firm goes public, his equity benefit will be in the many millions.

Needless to say, the final staging of his executive level negotiations didn't just happen. In the discussion that follows, the basics of our system are outlined in the most simple terms. If you don't have success, shift from the "present" and focus on the future: a review after six months, a better title, an automatic increase after time. These are easier things to get.

How to negotiate—a 7step system

Our staff is involved with negotiations at every level on a daily basis. We work on deals in every part of the country. This system is based on that experience and is a soft sell method that involves negotiating with skill and dignity. The advice has meant tens of thousands of dollars to many people.

1   Be sincere and reasonable... never cold or calculating

In the job-search situation, you're setting the tone for a long-term relationship. In fact, most people don't like negotiation because they associate it with confrontation and role playing, something that does not come naturally. The best negotiators are prepared and never cause irritation. Make sure to be sincere and reasonable, never cold or calculating.

As you approach your negotiations, you must have clear ideas about what you want. Realizing you will not achieve everything, keep your main objectives in mind, and never risk an entire negotiation by coming on too strong about less important points.

Of course, when you are ready to negotiate, the easiest way to "frame and strengthen" your position is to clarify that you

Look for strong buying signals from the employer, and be sure to never negotiate until the employer is sold on you. Our basic negotiating system is outlined on the following pages. Review it several times so that you can respond automatically when a situation arises.

have been exploring some other opportunities that also have a certain appeal.

2 Avoid premature income discussions

You need to avoid the hard lessons we see others experiencing every day. Here's an example. One client was a general manager with Exxon, earning a sizeable income, but wanting to win a new job at a 20% increase. After two meetings, the CEO said, *"Bill, we'd like to have you join us, and I'd like to work out something attractive for you. What have you been used to earning at Exxon?"*

At that point, having been encouraged, Bill explained his income. To make a long story short, he accepted a position. However, he later found out that the last person had been paid 40% more, and the company fully expected to match it.

Now, the moral is that you should never negotiate based on where you've been. Negotiation is like poker. You never want to lay your earnings on the table.

Premature discussions about money can be a real deal breaker. Besides, the more enthusiastic an employer becomes about you, the more likely he'll be willing to pay more.

Sometimes an interviewer will begin like this: *"Jim, before we get started, I'd like to know how much money you are looking for."* Here is a possible response: *"Charles, I could talk more intelligently about my circumstances after I know more about the job. Will this job have line responsibilities?"* **Or,** *"Charles, I would not take your time if I did not have a fairly good idea of the range you could pay. If we can agree that my experience fits your needs, I doubt we'll have a problem on compensation. My concern is whether your needs call for someone with my background."*

The idea is to be gracious while avoiding a direct answer. If an interviewer persists, say: *"I'd rather avoid discussing compensation. Challenge is most important to me, and I would like to talk money after we both feel I'm right for the job."* If all else fails, give a range surrounding your estimate of what the job pays.

3 Never commit when you get an offer

When offered a job, praise the firm and say you need some time to consider it. *"Charles, I am very pleased you made me an offer. This is an outstanding firm, and the position has great promise. I'm sure you can appreciate that I would like some time to give it further consideration. It would not present any problem, would it, if I get back to you on Monday?"*

Our standard recommendation for almost all clients is to get the offer in writing and ask for several days to respond. In some cases we advise people to respond slower or quicker depending on the situation. When you call back, open with some positive statements, then raise the possibility of redefining the job. *"Charles, with kids entering college, I had done some planning based on an income that was $10,000 higher. Would it be possible to take another look at the job specs? For my part, if you could make a modest additional investment, my performance will show you a handsome return. I sincerely hope that we can make some adjustment. Can we take a look at it?"*

Of course, if you are happy with the job, but would like to raise the salary, use the same technique, but show vulnerability, then suggest that a dollar figure be added to the base.

Normally, if that figure is within 15% of what you have been offered, the employer will not take offense and will grant you part of it. Of course, asking for more money is a negative, and needs to be balanced by positives. Consider the following: *"Charles, I cannot tell you how pleased I am. The challenge is there, and I think my experience is perfect. There is one problem, however. You see, one of the main reasons I wanted to make a change was for financial balance. Can you see your way clear to adding $10,000 to the base? It would ease my family situation considerably."*

4 Learn how to use vulnerability

Expressing a slight amount of vulnerability can be a powerful weapon. Just let the employer know that accepting the job as offered would cause you some personal difficulties. When you use this strategy, it plays to their desire to make you happy. Be flattered by the offer, but say that you may have to disappoint your family in order to afford the job:

"I love the job and really want to join you, but we'd have some difficulty because of the options I will be losing. Is there a chance you could go a little higher?"

Questioning, rather than demanding, is the rule. The best negotiators persuade through questions. This gives them needed information to gain control. It also gives them time to think and not put their cards on the table. Good negotiators will not say, *"I do not agree with you because…"* Rather, they will say, *"Charles, you do make a good point, but I wonder if there is room for another view."* They would never say, *"That would not be any good for me."* They might say, *"Charles, could you tell me how you think this would work for me?"*

Then they will follow up with questions, so the employer can discover that their proposal is not quite enough. If your questions lead them to discover they were wrong, they will be disposed to changing the terms.

5 Negotiate the job responsibilities

Reshape the job into a larger one, and the range will be higher. Begin with a positive comment about the job and the firm and suggest they might benefit by expanding responsibilities. Then share your thoughts.

For example, *"Charles, there is no doubt this is a good job. However, based on what you have told me, I could be even more helpful if a few related elements were added. There are three areas where my experience could make a difference. I'd like to discuss them so we can see if they could be included in the job description."*

You could then go on to talk about the areas where the firm might capitalize on your experience, showing with stories how you made contributions before. If the interviewer agrees these are important, have them added to the job description. Believe it or not, reshaping the job can often be just that simple. Can you see how we have applied basic principles here? There was no confrontation.

6 Introduce other things on which to base the offer

This can include the importance of the job to the firm, what you would make with a raise where you are, your total package, what you believe the market is for your background, or other offers you are considering.

In the example that follows, notice how there are no demands, only questions. By inviting employers to explore the situation, you are giving them the freedom to reach their own conclusions about whether their offer is too low. Using this approach, you come across as enthusiastic, sincere, and slightly vulnerable—never as cold or calculating, or as someone who is putting them in a corner. Your comment might be:

"Charles, let me first say once again how pleased I am over the offer. I feel very positive about the prospect of joining you, and my enthusiasm has continued to increase. This is the job I want. It's a situation where I could look forward to staying with you for the long term.

"There is one hurdle that I have to overcome. You see, I've been underpaid for some time, and it has created a situation where I need to start earning at a rate reflecting my ability to contribute. If I stayed where I am, I'd be due for a raise, which would come close to your offer.

"In looking at salary.com and talking with other firms, I've found that some realize this, and they have mentioned ranges that are 25% higher. Now, I don't want to work for them—I want to work for you. But I do have some pressing needs. Perhaps the firm could approve a higher offer. Can we pursue this together?"

7 Use your enthusiasm throughout

If you load maximum enthusiasm into your statements, it becomes nearly impossible for the employer to conclude that you should not be with them. Enthusiasm assumes even more importance when you have been underpaid. Ideally, an offer should be based on your value to the company, but in reality, most employers will base their offers on present earnings.

Things to consider negotiating

A contract. The following are usually incorporated: the length of the agreement, your specific assignment, your title, location, to whom you report, your compensation and what happens if there is a merger or if you are fired. It should also cover the specific items on the negotiation list that are part of your package. Any agreement you accept should cover all nonlegal situations under which an employer may choose to terminate you. Signing bonuses and generous severance packages are moving into all income levels—especially when there is a relocation.

Base salary. When you make a change, you want to expect a total package that is more than where you were. Elements include commissions, medical and life insurance, annual bonus based on meeting performance goals, profit sharing and pension plans. If you negotiate profit sharing, know the accounting.

Exit strategy... and outplacement assistance. Standard agreements cover six months' to a year's severance... triggered if the firm lessens your responsibilities. Regarding outplacement assistance, what you want to negotiate is a provision for private professional assistance for a period of up to six months... with you selecting the specific service provider of your choice.

Stock option purchase plans... and stock grants. If you purchase stock at market price, the company may buy an equal amount under your name up to a percentage of your income. With stock grants, you will most likely be obligated for taxes based upon the market value.

ISOs (incentive stock options). This is an option to purchase a certain number of shares at market value on a given day, generally exercisable years away. The primary value of ISOs is that should you eventually buy them, no tax is due on the day of purchase... as you pay only on your capital gains when your shares are sold.

Restricted stock units... phantom stock options and stock appreciation rights (SARs). Restricted stock units are pegged in value, e.g., as one share of stock for every five units. The key is when you can convert to cash or shares. Phantom stock options or SARs usually involve the difference in market value between the time granted and value when converted.

Non-qualified stock options. This is an option to purchase stock below market prices. Tax will be due on the difference between the price at which you exercise your right of purchase and the market value of the stock.

Relocation expenses and other perks. This can include house purchase, moving expenses, mortgage rate differential, real estate, closing costs, cost of bridge loan, trips to look for a home, lodging fees, tuition, and spouse reemployment services. These can include automobile lease, luncheons, athletic/country club membership, child care, physical exam, disability pay, legal assistance, product discounts, dining room privileges, financial planning assistance, tuition reimbursement, CPA and tax assistance, short-term loans, insurance benefits after termination, special reimbursement for foreign service, outplacement assistance and deferred compensation.

When you are persuading people, you're really helping them help themselves. They are already convinced that your joining the firm benefits them. When an offer is received... consider these negotiation goals:

■ See if you can get your job responsibilities expanded
■ Try to increase your initial salary offer by 10-30%
■ You want to secure benefits that are right for you
■ Negotiating a signing bonus of 10-25% is not unusual
■ Negotiating stock options / equity may be important to you

Negotiating sets the tone for your relationship.

Recapping this chapter. This system is easy to use and doesn't provoke confrontation. Avoid anything that might cause irritations and never be argumentative. Make sure you appear sincere and reasonable—never cold or calculating.

Quick action steps. Our professionals can and do play a key role here for clients, but just following these guidelines can have a major impact on what you can achieve. Follow the 7-step formula to the letter, and be sure to know what you want to negotiate.

"He's a businessman. I'll make him an offer he can't refuse."
—Mario Puzo in the Godfather, 1969

If you find yourself unemployed, just follow these suggestions and get into action fast.

When you are between jobs you have the extra time you need to run a truly aggressive search.

18 How to handle being unemployed

You can turn unemployment to your personal advantage.

As a group, virtually everyone who is unemployed eventually becomes reemployed, but some do it quickly, while others struggle, give up or settle for poor positions. With the right effort many can win new jobs that are more attractive than what they had and in healthy industries.

Experience has shown that as time passes, the less capable you will be (both psychologically and emotionally) to do what must be done to win a new job. So, the key is to have a schedule of full activity: meetings, interviews, letter writing, phone calls, follow-ups and negotiations. For action oriented people, being unemployed simply means having the time to do a lot of the things that need to be done. On the other hand, if they aren't active... many quickly get discouraged. Here are some observations.

1—Get support from your employer. Many employers are concerned about their people and want to provide help. With respect to severance, corporations will sometimes extend financial support or maintain benefits. Some firms will also extend outplacement counseling, if you think it would help.

Make sure there is total agreement on the reason for your separation. Work out an explanation that puts you in the best possible light. Once you have arranged for the best possible support, be prepared to explain why you are unemployed. You may be able to state that the termination was due to factors beyond anyone's control, such as a cutback, merger or reorganization.

Where it applies, make the point that the final separation was made at your initiative because you are a loyal person who gives 100%, and you did not want to look for a job while drawing a paycheck, or take a lesser position. And, be ready to provide references who will speak enthusiastically. Consider people you worked with, those who worked for you, customers, suppliers, or influential people in any part of the company.

Never imply threats. If you are in a position to harm your employer, they will know about it without your saying so, and they'll take it into account when they deal with you. It is to your advantage that your relationship remain positive. If you were terminated for performance, remind your employer that judgments about performance can be subjective, and point out that you could be seriously harmed by a negative reference.

2—Get your resumes created and build your knowledge. Review this book a number of times and really learn the content.

3—Get yourself a mentor and become "innovative." It can be anyone you respect. You need to share your progress with that person throughout your campaign. Also set aside one hour each morning to make a list of leads, ideas, and people to contact. Look for breaking news about any industries of interest.

4—Be active, proactive and maintain a winning attitude. Devote two hours a day to sending out letters or phone calling based on a plan of action, and work to arrange at least one interview or personal meeting. And, allow at least a half-hour each day for exercise. Positive thoughts are easier if you stay physically fit.

Common pitfalls when you're unemployed

Turning down your first offer. It should be given consideration. And, the same goes for temporary consulting.

Being unwilling to relocate. Sometimes it is better to go where new firms and industries are springing up. While it is difficult to leave, most people can adjust better than they realize.

Not accepting introductions. We've all heard it. "I'm not going to press myself on my friends." The truth is, most people want to help friends. It makes people feel good to know they've done something, however small, to support your efforts.

Feeling sorry for yourself. It is a normal reaction, but, who is being hurt by these emotions? The answer is you.

Holding out for unrealistic income. Consider a two-step move.

Allowing your health to slip. Attitude and physical fitness go hand in hand. It may be time to focus more on fitness.

Displaying a bad mood. The wrong attitude will alienate those who want to help you.

Allowing financial pressure to cause inertia. Financial pressures are often the toughest to withstand. Don't be afraid to borrow, or to take part-time or temporary work.

What some people say about unemployment

■ *"My advice to others would be to stay busy, be positive and feel good about yourself. I know it isn't the main purpose, but your system builds confidence and self esteem."*

■ *"I have been unemployed three times in my career. As a result, I have become somewhat of an expert. Building an entirely new will to succeed is the truly essential ingredient."*

■ *"If a person can build a will to succeed, then with your system it is only a matter of time. On the other hand, things won't go well if they dwell on the past."*

How to build and maintain a will to succeed

A positive attitude is the most common thread among all winners. It will separate you from the many who give up, settle for less, or stay in unattractive situations. It's easy to build a will to succeed if you follow some basic guidelines.

1—Develop positive beliefs. Now is a good time to remind yourself of all the good things you have done. Write down positive things "you've done and can do." Make it as long and complete as possible. You will find it reassuring. It will begin to provide reinforcement for the positive attitude you must maintain. For example: I have increased profits. I have attracted new business. I have cut costs, etc. Here are some "can do's" to consider: I can work with all levels of people. I can get things done quickly. I can motivate others, and so forth.

2—Get rid of negative beliefs. Having built a set of positive beliefs about yourself, your second step is to get rid of beliefs that might inhibit your will to succeed. Are you saying, "Things are bad, it's a grim world out there." If so, this simply reflects your beliefs about "the way you think things really are." If you believe the economy is bad, you will see breaking news and pay attention to layoffs or sales declines. On the other hand, if you believe that there are many areas of opportunity, then you will notice new firms, new products and the like.

3—Set your expectations high. Our expectations affect what happens to us. Obvious examples are the many sports teams and athletes who, when asked about their success, often reply, *"We expected all along that we would win."* A close look at the leaders in almost any field reveals a common theme. Whether it's a leading scientist, educator, salesperson, or leader of industry, each of them have had positive expectations of themselves.

4—Put positive expectations to work. For instance, if someone tells you that an interview can take only 15 minutes, recognize it's a screening interview and build expectations that it will allow you to showcase your potential. Here's another example: Suppose you had an excellent interview, called twice afterwards, and got no response. Don't assume they have lost interest. Instead, assume they're busy and that they are still very interested. Decide now that your second meeting will be better than the first. With that kind of expectation, you will then find it easy to write a short follow-up note that your interest continues to grow, and that you are dedicated to becoming the best ever in the job.

5—Project a positive attitude. Talk to people about your positive expectations. It reaffirms your commitment. Put yourself on the line. Let these ideas flow into your attitude. Work at this. It's easy and it's fun. A spring in your step, a firm handshake, a confident look in your eye, and comments that reveal a positive outlook can all help you project good feelings to the outside world.

6—Make things happen by getting into action. If you look at achievers in any field, you will find that they are very active. It's a simple fact that taking action is in itself like taking an energy tonic. Choose any kind of example you like. The head of a college breathing new life into an institution, a company president turning around firm, a coach turning a losing team into winners. They are so intent on their actions, there is no room for doubt and indecision. You can do the same thing.

"A positive mental attitude will create more miracles than any wonder drug."   *—Patricia Neal*

"There's no such thing as expecting too much."
                                                        —Susan Cheever

"It's not whether you get knocked down. It's whether you get back up."   *—Vince Lombardi*

Approach success as being inevitable. A positive attitude separates you from the pack. It's what all winners have. And, if you are unemployed, remember that you have time to do it right!

Be confident. Confidence is all about positive expectations for good things to happen. It affects your willingness to commit your energy, time and resources in pursuit of your search.

Have passion and drive. Passion and drive make a difference. It's the work ethic you bring to the table.

Be committed. This is influenced by your goals. So select goals that mean a lot and the pursuit will keep you committed.

Invest in yourself. There is no new product… and there is no new business… that can get started without some investment.

Take initiatives. One of the nice things about this system is you can be creative and take more actions than ever before.

Expect to win. In the end… with our system, it will all come back to confidence. Make succeeding a self-fulfilling prophecy.

Appendix 1
Unprecedented times.

As this book goes to press, for well over a year there has been a 24/7 spotlight on unemployment. There are also economists who foresee a very prolonged slow improvement. These predictions are not encouraging to job seekers. As pointed out in this book, job seekers need to start out with the brightest perspective possible, and a strong belief system. So let's look at some facts that will help you do that.

While unemployment remains high, the rate among college graduates is less than 50% of the national rate. Further, unemployment has been concentrated in industries that get huge publicity. Banking, construction, autos, heavy manufacturing, high-end consumer products, luxury retailing, mortgage banking and others have obviously borne the brunt.

But other industries are affected far less, or in some cases not at all. Biotechnology, healthcare, many technologically demanding products, clean energy, waste remediation, companies in many industries that have pioneered better products and services, suppliers for home gardens and local farming, and discount retailers are examples. IBM recorded record profits. Wal-Mart's success and that of "dollar stores" has been well publicized.

Smaller companies are not immune, but many are stable or hiring. In terms of who is recruiting, for the most part it is small companies with between 10 and 1,000 employees. This continues a trend in recent years, where the vast percentage of all new employment has come from small businesses.

As mentioned earlier, it's important to keep in mind that the overall size of the U.S. marketplace is largely determined by turnover. Positions become available because people retire... get terminated... go into their own businesses... or accept promotions outside of their current employer. This is what drives the job market.

Growth companies are very important to the marketplace. Every month there are examples of companies producing better revenues and profits than last year. They may not get the headlines that bad news commands, but the fact is that many smaller and mid-sized businesses are healthy and have not altered their growth plans for next year.

How long will slow employment last? No one knows, but probably for some time. For right now the job market in many industries remains on the same trendline as it was a year ago.

Since the job market is driven by turnover, the total number of job seekers in the market is affected by the bad news that is so prominently reported. The market itself is normally dominated by employed people who normally are in search of new or better jobs. And, the average person changes positions once every 4 years in the U.S.

In negative financial times... the number of employed people who look for jobs... generally declines. The constant media barrage causes many people to feel thankful they have decent positions, and they postpone their thoughts about bettering themselves... until they think the job market has improved.

This actually makes for a positive opportunity for those who need to find new employment or who are motivated to advance themselves. To put this into perspective, here is a small example. We know that in the U.S. approximately 3.8 million people secure jobs at $100,000 or above each year.

The government knows this based upon their tax filings the subsequent year. At the same time, it is generally estimated that upwards of 25 million people each year seek new positions at this level. Most discontinue their efforts and stay where they are.

During a worsening economic climate, these statistics will fluctuate. However, the main focus should be on what the climate does for your competitive chances. This year, instead of 3.8 million securing jobs at $100,000, perhaps only 3.5 or 3.6 million will. On the other side of the coin, it is likely that the number seeking new positions at this level would dramatically be reduced. This could drop from 25 million to 20 million. The net result is that there is less competition for the jobs that are available.

"The truth of the matter is that you always know the right thing to do. The hard part is doing it."
—General Norman Schwarzkopf

Appendix 2
Classical career situations.

While each career is unique, there are certain common situations that exist. If you fall into one of them, the following discussion will give you some guidance.

Are you a young executive moving up?

These executives are typically 28-46 years old, B.A./B.S. or M.B.A., doing well financially, either highly marketable and confident... or concerned because they have been blocked for some time.

Many of these people are at an important crossroads. And many potentially great careers are lost at this critical stage. Some, of course, are highly marketable. It's important for these executives to explore *all* their options when making a move... not just one or two. On the other hand, some executives are less confident. Some fail to discover the importance of broadening out before it's too late. Age can be a factor here. They're well aware of the bottlenecks that may prevent their growth where they are.

Some are in situations where they have not attracted attention from top management. Other talented people may be just ahead of them—or they may not be aligned well enough politically. Because they value their careers so highly, a bad move at this stage can be tragic. They must make the right move. Here, one of the keys is to uncover and market their full range of assets and transferable skills.

If these people don't control their career direction, they may lose the advantage of their good beginnings. Others are facing a marketability decline. These people are often wise to consider new environments in smaller and medium-sized firms, and in emerging industries—where they can receive greater responsibility.

Working in an entrepreneurial environment and combining it with large corporate experience can be an excellent platform for future moves. Or, it could be time for some to take a calculated risk to make a dramatic move up financially. They are ready to do their boss's job... and perhaps much better.

People like this have often made the mistake of just dabbling in the market... answering ads, speaking with a few recruiters. The trouble is, that while they might have surfaced something sooner or later, it would only have been one offer—requiring a one-shot leap of faith.

For these people, having a structured system for developing the right interviews is critical. Good numbers are necessary because executives have to be realistic about rejections. And, the higher you go, the truer this is.

Are you an officer with a limited future?

The corporate officer—$100K to $750K+... age 36 to 62... is often at the peak of his / her marketability. Their job is threatened, the challenge is gone, or they have been terminated.

People in this position are often unsure about their futures. Normally in control, they sense changes ahead. A few may be concerned that they have wasted their best career opportunity. Others may be fed up with politics and want out entirely. Some worry their careers could be lost.

At higher levels, these people are often concerned about campaigning with dignity. They also feel that they cannot afford to make another mistake. Their next move often needs to be their last. Time may be their greatest enemy. There is a tendency for these professionals to have an exaggerated view of their marketability— thinking it is easier than it is... or that their network will produce the right opportunity. Instead, they need to plan on getting much wider exposure than they may have realized.

Have you had too many previous jobs?

Often, a person will come to us after several bad moves. Emotionally, they may be confused, and despite talent, they are doubting themselves.

Typically, this is where an executive is concerned and wondering if there is any hope. Is the problem with them, or are they a victim of circumstances? In this situation, if you examine your previous changes, you may see that bad moves in the past were made because you didn't professionally search. You took situations that just came your way. At this stage, you need to control your career destiny. Mistakes must be avoided and a move made on a more scientific basis.

Historically, many in this situation have overreacted against past problems by taking the first thing that came along. For most people in this position, the key to success will rest in their ability to generate a lot of interviews. Then they can be selective, accept the right situation and stay with it.

Have you been too long in one firm or industry?

These people do not know what they are worth and may never have looked before. For this reason, the ability to expand their true marketability is paramount. Unless their lethargy is shaken, they may spend the best years of their lives with indecision. Action for them may come too late to be meaningful.

Most of the time, these people are unaware of what's really out there for them. Not only are they unaware of what's out there, but employers will be ignorant of their value, because they have never prepared materials to present their full story. And whenever there's a problem of ignorance, the solution is communication.

If you are in this category, the weight of your campaign will fall on your ability to build an appropriate bridge, from where you've been—to where you want to be... both through your resumes and communication in general. I get concerned that in this category, the longer some wait, the more difficult the search may be.

Are you an entrepreneur entering the market?

These executives recognize that certain employers will be hesitant to hire them. They know there will be concerns about whether they may go back into their own business, and whether they can be a team player in a corporate structure.

Talented as they may be, former entrepreneurs face special challenges. Many are identified with a narrow industry, and they lack credibility outside that niche. Of course, some want, or need by virtue of non-compete agreements, to seek out positions in different industries. However, they are unsure of where they would fit. Some, having achieved success, want to be in a business that has an explicit mission of enriching people's lives.

If you are in this category, this is a critical move. You have not done this before, and you need to do it right. Chances are you are also a down-to-earth realist. To have credibility, you must have concrete "selling propositions," as well as "industry hooks" based on facts and the realities of the marketplace, not just vague generalities. Entrepreneurs are seldom short on achievements. However, what you need the most are powerful written presentations that make you credible over a broader spectrum.

Appendix 3
When should you launch a search?

What makes national news about the market may have little to do with the reception you get in the marketplace. Surprising as it may seem, through good economies and bad, the total number of employed Americans is sure to increase over the long term. Furthermore, the openings available depend more on turnover than anything else... people who retire, leave or get terminated, thereby creating a job opening.

Another thing to keep in mind is that some people are in career situations that will only get worse if they don't take action. The longer you wait to make a decision, the worse your situation may become.

The longer a person remains on the brink of losing a job, unhappy every day, under stress or unchallenged, the deeper the hole that person may dig for themselves. If you wait and allow this to happen, the negative impact on your mental outlook can be severe. You will never be able to approach marketing yourself with the right frame of mind.

Then there are some liabilities that only get worse with time. If you have topped out, or stayed in one industry or one company for a long time, you will get increasingly less marketable. Of course, age clearly gets more challenging with time. Things will only be more serious later on. You also need to concern yourself with your achievements that may have been significant, but which can lose their impact. As time goes on, the power of those earlier achievements will become less and less. With senior executives and high achievers, the impact factor is very important.

Appendix 4
Your destiny is in your hands.

With this system there might be a temptation to think that little effort is required to win an attractive job. We wish that everyone could experience that. But through our regular staff communications with thousands of job seekers, we have statistics that tell us otherwise.

What we have found is that to make our system work, clients must use this advice aggressively. Of our most successful clients… people who succeeded in a minimum of time… 92% devoted a great many hours to their search. And, when we looked at the campaigns of people whose search took longer than expected, most had not taken aggressive advantage of our system.

The implications are clear. Similar to any other resources you might use to help you achieve a goal, no matter how effective they might have been for thousands of others, they will work for you only if you use them in the manner that was intended.

Attending *"the finest golf school"* will not lower your score unless you practice regularly. The most effective *"weight loss program"* works only if you adhere to what it requires. The most rigorous *"physical conditioning program"* gets you in great shape only if you get to the gym and do the exercises.

So, it's up to you to make the most of this system. That means searching for your new job on a daily basis, and finding information to make certain interview-producing actions work, and being creative and aggressive in surfacing the right opportunities for you.

Appendix 5
Will this system work for everyone?

No. This system is for the vast majority of individuals anywhere who feel they have a record of achievement at professional, managerial or executive levels. There are few professionals who could not dramatically increase their chances by aggressively using this system. But, some start out with such a high degree of difficulty, that even with the leverage provided, they stand a less than average chance for success. For example:

▶ People seeking relocation, but with no budget to travel to a new location for interviews

▶ People with very narrow geographical requirements in small second-tier markets

▶ People who are not legal to work in the U.S.

▶ Those with extreme specialization

▶ Those with a severe disability that prevents them from interviewing or speaking easily

▶ Those with poor education credentials and limited achievements to compensate

▶ Those with significant age issues and no record of valuable contributions in demand today

▶ People who are simply not motivated, and

▶ Some who face bias due to personality, appearance, language problems, or depression

People in these categories need to consider that while our system will enhance anyone's chances, their odds for success will still not be favorable.

There is a major difference in "how long" job hunting takes with traditional methods... vs. people using this system.

	Traditional	This system Average	This system Aggress'v
Scientific	12.8 mo's	4.4 mo's	3.4 mo's
General mgmt.	12.7 mo's	4.2 mo's	3.4 mo's
Legal / consulting	10.6 mo's	4.2 mo's	3.3 mo's
Human resources	10.9 mo's	3.9 mo's	3.2 mo's
Accounting / finance	9.9 mo's	3.9 mo's	3.2 mo's
Misc. staff positions	9.9 mo's	3.8 mo's	3.2 mo's
Operations	9.9 mo's	3.5 mo's	3.1 mo's
Administrative	9.4 mo's	3.5 mo's	3.0 mo's
Marketing / sales / PR	8.8 mo's	3.5 mo's	2.9 mo's
Engineering & related	7.3 mo's	3.3 mo's	2.9 mo's
Information systems	7.1 mo's	3.1 mo's	2.8 mo's

These statistics are general data. And, as with any generalized data, you need to be cautious in assessing this relative to your own situation. With our survey of those using this system, the length of campaigns varied widely with the level of income, their transferable skills and other credentials. People in mainstream fields *(accounting, finance, sales, marketing, operations, etc.)* obviously moved faster than did specialists.

In addition, those seeking major industry changes take longer. However, results will vary most with the aggressiveness of people's searches. Listed in the last column are statistics for people who said they aggressively used our suggestions relative to following an action plan, direct mail, leads to emerging opportunities and networking with personal marketing websites. Not covered by this data is any consideration of the actual quality of the position that was accepted.

About Advanced Career Technologies and personal marketing.

Originally we were a dot com. The executives who organized our firm included a group of highly experienced professionals... all of whom had prior experience in recruiting, outplacement or career services. Our common bond was a desire to create new technology and personal services to help job seekers.

We knew that for more than 30 years, professionals had been using the same approaches to look for a new job. With this in mind, our starting point was to begin developing technology that would connect jobs seekers to the openings, leads and contacts they needed—all in one place.

We formed a division we call Job Market Access Center... or JMAC for short. It took a venture capital investment of more than $30,000,000 and several years to develop.

Here's why we've focused on new innovations in this field. You may be surprised to know that the U.S. Labor Department has said it now takes the average professional... 9 to 12 months to find a new position.

Fortune Magazine... has now had three cover stories over several years... all of which documented the long journey people face and their strain and worry. *The Chicago Tribune* has also done many articles. One survey said that of people who lost their jobs... only 5%... or 1 in 20... get back to their previous level of responsibility. We're not certain that this is the case... but we are certain that in many situations, it doesn't need to happen.

Many people claim the job markets have now changed more in the last five years than in the previous 30. And we agree. The bottom line is, an enormous need has emerged for better ways to search for a job. And, that is where our mission comes in.

Here are some other applications where technology has facilitated a new way to change jobs. An early challenge was to develop an information gathering system that would work on-line, one that would surface all aspects of a person's background and experiences—regardless of their location. We now do this through our online *Career History and Marketability Profile.*

Knowing the importance of transferable skills, our staff created a proprietary "marketability checklist." Once you complete this profile, your marketability report is instantly available online, comparing you on a statistical basis to 2,000 others in your income range.

The Internet also enabled us to introduce a new concept, the personal marketing website. It multiplies the power of networking many times over, as it adds substantially to the number of contacts you can make in a job search.

Consider these other innovations made possible by the Internet and new technology. Just a few years ago, who would have dreamed that anywhere in the world you could receive instant access to almost 97% of all published professional jobs—*all in one place?*

Through JMAC we can now put this information at your fingertips. And, who would have imagined that you could have emails streamed to you... giving the daily events that signal emerging jobs in your metro area... and in your industries of interest? Going even further, who would have thought you could have your credentials quickly placed with your highest probability prospects in more than 230 countries?

Not mentioned above, we've also pioneered software to isolate new industry options that should be pursued... and new ways to prepare people worldwide for interviewing. The need to provide expensive outplacement seminars was also eliminated as we condensed 3-day workshops into 15 fast moving and short online audios as part of our Job Market Access Center.

Even more important, other software allows us to provide people with market intelligence on employers, including backgrounds on decision makers, and much more.

Throughout our development, we've also been assembling online the best advice for every job search situation, culled from thousands of successful searches. All of these innovations will themselves lead the way to continued further positive developments for faster and easier ways to run a job search.